Knitting in the Round

Edited by Jeanne Stauffer

Exclusively using Plymouth yarns

Creative Consultant: Uyvonne Bigham of Plymouth Yarn Co.

HOUSE of
WHITE
BIRCHES

PUBLISHERS
SINCE 1947

Knitting in the Round

Editor: Jeanne Stauffer
Associate Editor: Dianne Schmidt
Technical Editor: Diane Zangl
Copy Editors: Conor Allen, Michelle Beck, Nicki Lehman

Photography: Tammy Christian, Christena Green, Kelly Heydinger
Photography Stylist: Tammy Nussbaum

Publishing Services Manager: Brenda Gallmeyer
Book & Cover Design: Edith Teegarden
Graphic Artist: Pam Gregory
Production Assistant: Marj Morgan
Technical Artist: Chad Summers
Art Director: Brad Snow

Chief Executive Officer: John Robinson
Publishing Director: David Mckee
Book Marketing Director: Craig Scott
Editorial Director: Vivian Rothe

Printed in the United States of America
First Printing: 2004
Library of Congress Number: 2004105970
ISBN: 1-59217-039-0

Every effort has been made to ensure the accuracy and completeness of the instructions
in this book. However, we cannot be responsible for human error or for the results when using
materials other than those specified in the instructions, or for variations in individual work.

Retail outlet owners and resellers: For additional copies of this book call (800) 772-6643.

1 2 3 4 5 6 7 8 9

A Note From The Editor

When I started knitting, I used only straight needles because that's what I was taught to use. After a few years, I soon discovered the joy of using circular needles, especially for large projects like afghans. In my case, I had to cast on over 300 stitches for a cape.

Because someone told me how difficult it is to use double-pointed needles, I never tried them for many years. I would look for a similar pattern that used circular or straight needles. Finally, I had enough confidence in my knitting ability to try double-pointed needles. They did feel awkward at first, but soon I was just knitting along, the same as I do with circular and straight needles. Really, it wasn't hard.

More recently, a new employee wanted to learn to knit and the project she wanted to make required her to use double-pointed needles. We didn't tell her that double-pointed needles were difficult or even unusual in any way. Guess what happened? Since she didn't know double-pointed needles are difficult to work with, she didn't have any trouble, even though this was just her second knitting project ever. She thought that double-pointed needles were just different; not difficult.

With circular and double-pointed needles, you'll discover the pleasure of having fewer seams to sew at the end. With larger projects, you won't have long straight needles poking out to the side. Once you take a look at the projects in this book, you won't want to find similar projects. You'll want to dive right in and start knitting in the round.

Warm regards,

CONTENTS

Knitting in the Round With Circular Needles

New Terms & Abbreviations

Pm: place marker

Rnd(s): round(s)

Working end: the end of the yarn that is attached to the ball

You've been knitting things back and forth on straight needles, turning at the end of every row. How would you like to just knit, round after round, without turning at all, and then have no seams to sew up when you are finished knitting?

You can! A method called circular knitting makes tubes of knitting in any size. You can make hats, socks, mittens and sweaters this way.

To knit on circular needles:

Photo 1

Photo 2

Photo 3

Photo 4

Right-hand Instructions

Step 1: Cast on the desired number of stitches onto the needle just as you would onto straight needles. Start practicing with a 16-inch circular needle. You need to have enough stitches to fill the needle.

Step 2: Spread the stitches evenly across the needle, and make sure they are not twisted. (Photo 1)

Step 3: Hold the needles so the working end of yarn is on the right-hand tip of the needle, and the first stitch you cast on is on the left-hand tip of the needle. (Photo 2)

Step 4: Place a stitch marker on the RH needle. The marker is between the first and last stitch you cast on and marks the beginning of a round. Stitch markers can be a loop of yarn in a contrasting color or a purchased plastic stitch marker. (Photo 3)

Step 5: Using the working end, knit the first stitch on the left-hand needle. This is the first stitch you cast on. (Photo 4)

In patterns, Steps 2–5 are usually called "join, being careful not to twist."

Step 6: Keep knitting all the stitches, sliding them along the needle as you work them from the left tip to the right tip.

Step 7: When you reach the stitch marker, slip it to the right-hand needle, then keep knitting.

Step 8: Keep knitting round and round until your tube is as long as you need. (Photo 5)

Photo 5

Right-hand Instructions

To knit on four double-pointed needles:

Step 1: Cast all the stitches onto one needle.

Step 2: Slide one third of the stitches onto each of two other needles. (Photo 1)

Step 3: Make sure the stitches are straight across all the needles; then fold the two end needles around so the last stitch cast on and the first stitch cast on are next to each other, with the working end on the right. (Photo 2)

Step 4: Insert the tip of the fourth needle into the first stitch you cast on. (Photo 3) Use the working end of yarn to knit all the stitches across this needle. (Photo 4)

Step 5: Now use the needle that just became free to knit all the stitches off the next needle.

Step 6: Keep knitting around, using the free needle to knit stitches off the next needle in line. (Photo 5)

Although it looks tricky because there are so many needles, it's not hard at all. You are only knitting from one needle to another just as you have been doing all along!

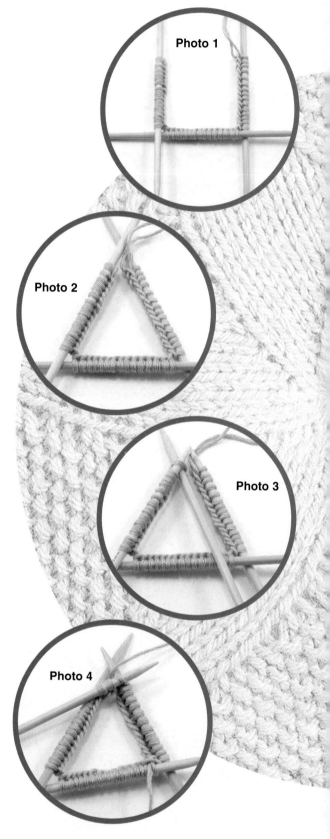

Photo 1

Photo 2

Photo 3

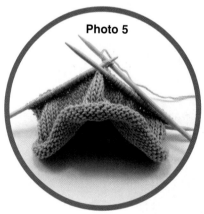

Photo 5

Photo 4

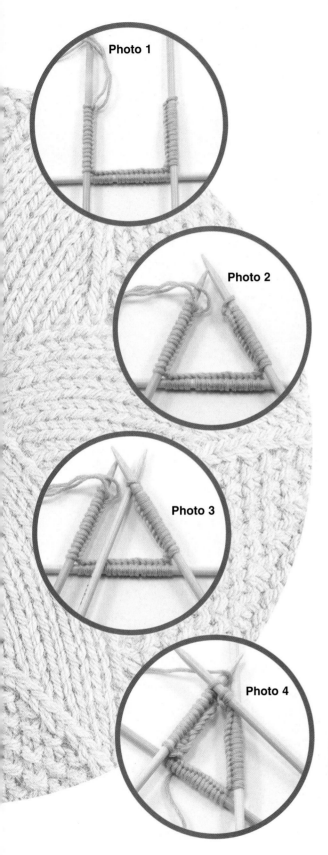

Photo 1

Photo 2

Photo 3

Photo 4

Left-hand Instructions

Note: *Left-handed knitters should try knitting right-handed first. For those who cannot knit right-handed, we've included left-hand instructions.*

To knit on four double-pointed needles:

Step 1: Cast all the stitches onto one needle.

Step 2: Slide one third of the stitches onto each of two other needles. (Photo 1)

Step 3: Make sure the stitches are straight across all the needles; then fold the two end needles around so the last stitch cast on and the first stitch cast on are next to each other, with the working end on the right. (Photo 2)

Step 4: Insert the tip of the fourth needle into the first stitch you cast on. (Photo 3) Use the working end of yarn to knit all the stitches across this needle. (Photo 4)

Step 5: Now use the needle that just became free to knit all the stitches off the next needle.

Step 6: Keep knitting around, using the free needle to knit stitches off the next needle in line. (Photo 5)

Although it looks tricky because there are so many needles, it's not hard at all. You are only knitting from one needle to another just as you have been doing all along! ●

Photo 5

Comfy
Wrap-Arounds

Is there anything more comfortable than being wrapped up in a cozy knitted throw? Or having a soft knitted pillow under your head? You'll enjoy knitting these afghans and pillows knowing what awaits you.

Wrapped Stitch Diagonals

Design by Kathy Cheifetz

Long stitches are the basis for the interesting cables in a cozy afghan.

Skill Level

INTERMEDIATE

Finished Size

Approx 46 x 60 inches

Materials

[4 MEDIUM] Plymouth Encore 75 percent acrylic/25 percent wool worsted weight yarn (200 yds/100g per skein): 15 skeins mulberry heather #355

- Size 15 (10mm) 32-inch circular needle or size needed to obtain gauge
- Cable needle
- Size M/13 (9mm) crochet hook

Gauge

13 sts and 12 rows = 4 inches/10cm in Wrapped Diagonal pat with 2 strands of yarn held tog

To save time, take time to check gauge.

Special Abbreviations

LS (Long Stitch): Wrap yarn around needle twice purlwise.

WC (Wrapped Cable): Place next (long) stitch on cn and hold in front dropping extra wrap, k3, k1 from cn.

Pattern Stitch

Wrapped Diagonal

Row 1 and all WS rows: *K1, p3, LS, k1, p5; rep from *, end last rep k1, p3, LS, k1.

Rows 2, 4, 6, 20, 22, and 24: *P1, WC, p6; rep from *, end last rep p1, WC, p1.

Rows 8, 10, 12, 14, 16 and 18: *P1, WC, p1, k5; rep from *, end last rep p1, WC, p1.

Rep Rows 7–24 for pat.

Pattern Notes

Two strands of yarn are held together for entire afghan.

Circular needle is used to accommodate large number of sts. Do not join; work in rows.

Afghan

With 2 strands of yarn held tog, cast on 149 sts.

Work Rows 1–24 of Wrapped Diagonal pat once, [work Rows 7–24] 10 times.

Work Rows 20–24 once.

Bind off on WS without working extra wraps.

Finishing

With RS facing using crochet hook and 2 strands of yarn held tog, work 1 sl st loosely in every other st or row around entire afghan, working a ch-1 at each corner. ●

Mirage Afghan & Bolster

Designs by Carol May

Just as in a shimmering desert mirage, the squares in this set appear then disappear by changing into stripes. It all depends on how you look at it.

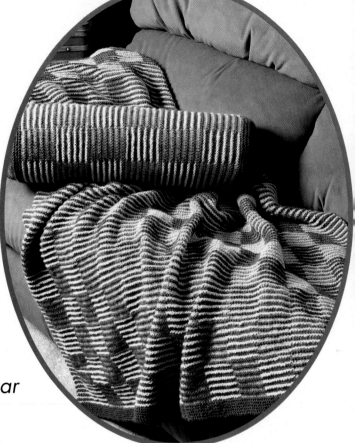

Skill Level

BEGINNER

Finished Size

Afghan: Approx 45 x 60 inches

Bolster: 7 inches diameter x 23 inches long

Materials

Plymouth Encore 75 percent acrylic/25 percent wool worsted weight yarn (200 yds/100g per skein): Afghan: 6 skeins dark green #1233 (A), 5 skeins light green #1231 (B); Bolster: 2 skeins (A), 1 skein (B)

- Size 7 (4.5mm) 16- and 24-inch circular needles or size needed to obtain gauge
- Size I/9 (5.5mm) crochet hook
- Purchased batting for double-size quilt

Gauge

20 sts and 34 rows = 4 inches/10cm in Mirage pat

To save time, take time to check gauge.

Pattern Stitches

Mirage (when worked in rows)

Row 1 and all RS rows: With A, knit.

Rows 2, 6, 10, 14, 18 and 22: With B, *k12, p12; rep from * across.

Rows 4, 8, 12, 16 and 20: With A, *p12, k12; rep from * across.

Row 24: With A, knit.

Rows 26, 30, 34, 38, 42 and 46: With B, *p12, k12; rep from * across.

Rows 28, 32, 36, 40, and 44: With A, *k12, p12; rep from * across.

Row 48: With A, knit.

Rep Rows 1–48 for pat.

Mirage (when worked in rnds)

Rnd 1 and all uneven-numbered rnds: With A, knit.

Rnds 2, 6, 10, 14, 18 and 22: With B, *k12, p12; rep from * around.

Rnds 4, 8, 12, 16 and 20: With A, *p12, k12; rep from * around.

Rnd 24: With A, purl.

Rnds 26, 30, 34, 38, 42 and 46: With B, *p12, k12; rep from * around.

Rnds 28, 32, 36, 40, and 44: With A, *k12, p12; rep from * around.

Rnds 48: With A, purl.

Rep Rnds 1–48 for pat.

Pattern Notes

Colors are carried up work; do not cut after each row/round.

For afghan, bring new yarn under old to create an even edge.

Placing markers after every 12 sts of pattern will make it easier to work.

Eight sts at each end of afghan are kept in garter st border.

Afghan

With A and longer needle, cast on 304 sts loosely.

Work even in garter st for 12 rows.

Set up pat: K8, pm, [work Row 1 of Mirage pat] 12 times, pm, k8.

Keeping 8 sts at each end in garter st, and rem sts in established pat, work even until afghan measures approx 58 inches, ending with Row 24 or 48 of pat.

With A, work in garter st for 12 rows.

Bind off loosely; do not block.

Bolster

With A and shorter needle, cast on 96 sts loosely. Join without twisting, pm between first and last st.

Work even in garter st for 6 rnds.

Eyelet rnd: *K2tog, yo; rep from * around.

Work in St st for 3 inches, then in garter st for 6 rnds.

Beg with Rnd 2, work even in Mirage pat until bolster measures 23 inches above plain area.

Change to A and work in garter st for 6 rnds, then in St st for 3 inches.

Eyelet rnd: *K2tog, yo; rep from * around.

Work in garter st for 6 rnds.

Bind off loosely.

Cords
Make 2

With crochet hook and 2 strands of A held tog, make a 12-inch ch.

Finishing

Roll batting tightly to form a shape 23 inches long and 7 inches in diameter.

Place bolster over batting.

Thread 1 cord through each Eyelet rnd and tie tightly. ●

Carnival Blanket

Design by Barbara Venishnick

Add a highly textured yarn to the colors of Carnival and you have a gala celebration in the form of this afghan.

Skill Level

■■■□ INTERMEDIATE

Finished Size

Approx 40 x 45 inches

Materials

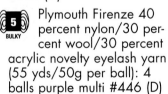 Plymouth Dreambaby DK 50 percent microfiber/50 percent nylon DK weight yarn (183 yds/ 50g per ball): 7 balls purple #112 (A), 2 balls each fuchsia #116 (B) and orange #114 (C)

Plymouth Firenze 40 percent nylon/30 percent wool/30 percent acrylic novelty eyelash yarn (55 yds/50g per ball): 4 balls purple multi #446 (D)

- Size 7 (4.5mm) 24- and (3) 40-inch circular needles or size needed to obtain gauge
- Stitch markers
- Size G/6 (4mm) crochet hook

Gauge

20 sts and 25 rows = 4 inches/10cm in Central Panel color pat

To save time, take time to check gauge.

Special Abbreviations

M1 (Make 1): Increase by lifting running strand between st just worked and next st onto LH needle, knit this st.

PT (Purl Twice): Purl 1, wrapping yarn twice around needle.

Pattern Notes

Circular needles are used to accommodate large number of sts. Do not join; work in rows.

For outside border, use 3 long circular needles, 2 to hold sts and 1 as a working needle.

Work all slipped sts with yarn in back.

Blanket

Central Panel

With A and shorter needle, cast on 77 sts.

Rows 1, 3 and 5 (RS): K6 B, [k5 A, k5 B] 7 times, k1 B.

Rows 2, 4 and 6: P6 B, [p5 A, p5 B] 7 times, p1 B.

Rows 7, 9 and 11: K6 A, [k5 C, k5 A] 7 times, k1 A.

Rows 8, 10 and 12: P6 A, [p5 C, p5 A] 7 times, p1 A.

[Rep Rows 1–12] 10 times.

Outer Border

With A and circular needle, k 77 sts, mark first and last sts for corners, pick up and k 99 sts evenly spaced along left edge of central panel, 77 sts along cast-on edge of central panel, mark first and last of these sts for corners, pick up and k 99 sts evenly spaced along right

edge of central panel, pm for beg of rnd. (352 sts)

Rnd 1: With A, [k1, p75, k1, p99] twice.

Rnd 2: With C, [k1, M1, knit to next marked st, M1] 4 times. (360 sts)

Rnd 3: With C, [k1, purl to next marked st] 4 times.

Rnds 4 and 5: With D, rep Rnds 2 and 3.

Rnds 6 and 7: With B, rep Rnds 2 and 3.

Rnds 8 and 9: With A, rep Rnds 2 and 3.

Rnd 10: With C, rep Rnd 2.

Rnd 11: With C, k1, [PT, p5] 14 times, PT, k1, [PT, p5] 18 times, PT, k1, [PT, p5] 14 times, PT, k1, [PT, p5] 18 times, PT.

Rnd 12: With D, k1, M1, *[sl 1 releasing double wrap, k5] 14 times, sl 1 releasing double wrap, M1, k1, M1, [sl 1 releasing double wrap, k5] 18 times, sl 1 releasing double wrap, M1, k1, M1; rep from * once, end M1.

Rnd 13: With D, k2, [sl 1, k5] 14 times, sl 1, k3, [sl 1, k5] 18 times, sl 1, k3, [sl 1, k5] 14 times, sl 1, k3, [sl 1, k5] 18 times, sl 1, k1.

Rnd 14: With D, k1, M1, k1, [sl 1, k5] 14 times, sl 1, [k1, M1] twice, k1, [sl 1, k5] 18 times, sl 1, [k1, M1] twice, k1, [sl 1, k5] 14 times, sl 1, [k1, M1] twice, k1, [sl 1, k5] 18 times, sl 1, k1, M1.

Rnd 15: With D, k3, *sl 1, k5; rep from *, end last rep sl 1, k2. (408 sts)

Rnds 16 and 17: With C, rep Rnds 2 and 3.

Rnds 18–49: With A, rep rnds 2 and 3. (544 sts)

Rnd 50: With B, rep Rnd 2.

Rnd 51: With B, *k1, [PT, p5] 26 times, PT, k1, [PT, p5] 30 times, PT; rep from * once.

Rnd 52: With D, *k1, M1, [sl 1 releasing double wrap, k5] 26 times, sl 1 releasing double wrap, M1, k1, M1, [sl 1 releasing double wrap, k5] 30 times, sl 1 releasing double wrap, M1; rep from * once.

Rnd 53: With D, k2, [sl 1, k5] 26 times, sl 1, k3, [sl 1, k5] 30 times, sl 1, k3, [sl 1, k5] 26 times, sl 1, k3, [sl 1, k5] 30 times, sl 1, k1.

Rnd 54: With D, k1, M1, k1, [sl 1, k5] 26 times, sl 1, [k1, M1] twice, k1, [sl 1, k5] 30 times, sl 1, [k1, M1] twice, k1, [sl 1, k5] 26 times, sl 1, [k1, M1] twice, k1, [sl 1, k5] 30 times, sl 1, k1, M1.

Rnd 55: With D, k3, *sl 1, k5; rep from *, end last rep sl 1, k2. (568 sts)

Rnds 56 and 57: With B, rep Rnds 2 and 3.

Rnds 58–61: With A, rep Rnds 2 and 3. (592 sts)

Rnd 62: Rep Rnd 2.

Rnd 63: With C, k1, [PT, p5] 28 times, PT, k1, [PT, p5] 32 times, PT, k1, [PT, p5] 28 times, PT, k1, [PT, p5] 32 times, PT.

Rnd 64: With D, *k1, M1, [sl 1 releasing double wrap, k5] 28 times, sl 1 releasing double wrap, M1, k1, M1, [sl 1 releasing double wrap, k5] 32 times, sl 1 releasing double wrap, M1; rep from * once.

Rnd 65: With D, k2, [sl 1, k5] 28 times, sl 1, k3, [sl 1, k5] 32 times, sl 1, k3, [sl 1, k5] 28 times, sl 1, k3, [sl 1, k5] 32 times, sl 1, k1.

Rnd 66: With D, k1, M1, k1, [sl 1, k5] 28 times, sl 1, [k1, M1] twice, k1, [sl 1, k5] 32 times, sl 1, [k1, M1] twice, k1, [sl 1, k5] 28 times, sl 1, [k1, M1] twice, k1, [sl 1, k5] 32 times, sl 1, k1, M1.

Rnd 67: With D, k3, *sl 1, k5; rep from *, end last rep sl 1, k2. (616 sts)

Rnds 68 and 69: With C, rep Rnds 2 and 3.

Rnds 70 and 71: With A, rep Rnds 2 and 3.

Rnds 72 and 73: With B, rep Rnds 2 and 3.

Rnds 74 and 75: With D, rep Rnds 2 and 3.

Rnds 76 and 77: With C, rep Rnds 2 and 3.

Rnds 78 and 79: With A, rep Rnds 2 and 3. (664 sts)

Bind off round: Hold colors A, B and C in left hand.

With crochet hook, draw a lp of A through first st, take st off needle, draw a lp of B through next st on needle and previous A st to bind off, draw a lp of A through next st and previous B st to bind off.

Keeping a loose tension, continue in this fashion working color sequence A, B, A, C, until all sts have been bound off. ●

Golden Lattice

Design by Sandi Prosser

Caramel and cream combine in a slipstitch motif that is reminiscent of the lattice patterns found on old-fashioned ice cream dishes.

Skill Level

EASY

Finished Size

Approx 38 x 48 inches

Materials

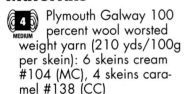 Plymouth Galway 100 percent wool worsted weight yarn (210 yds/100g per skein): 6 skeins cream #104 (MC), 4 skeins caramel #138 (CC)

- Size 7 (4.5mm) 29-inch circular needle

Gauge

18 sts and 42 rnds = 4 inches/10cm in Lattice pat

To save time, take time to check gauge.

Special Abbreviation

PU1 (Pick Up 1): Insert point of RH needle under loose strand of slip stitches 3 rounds below and knit it together with next stitch.

Pattern Stitch

Lattice

Rnd 1: With CC, knit.

Rnd 2: With CC, k2, *sl 5 wyif, k1; rep from * to last st, k1.

Rnds 3 and 4: With MC, knit.

Rnd 5: With CC, k1, sl 3, PU1, *sl 5, PU1; rep from * to last 4 sts, sl 3, k1.

Rnd 6: With CC, k1, sl 3 wyif, k1, *sl 5 wyif, k1; rep from * to last 4 sts, sl 3 wyif, k1.

Rnds 7 and 8: With MC, knit.

Rnd 9: With CC, k1, PU1, *sl 5, PU1; rep from * to last st, k1.

Rnd 10: With CC, k2, *sl 5 wyif, k1; rep from * to last st, k1.

Rep Rnds 3–10 for pat.

Pattern Notes

Throw is worked in the round with a steek; keep steek sts in p throughout entire throw.

Steek sts are not included in st counts.

Sl all sts purlwise.

Throw

With CC, cast on 177 sts, pm, cast on 4 sts for steek, pm. Join without twisting.

Work even in Lattice pat until throw measures approx 46 inches, ending with Rnd 5 or 9 of pat.

With CC, knit 1 rnd.

Bind off.

Sew and cut steek.

Side Border

With CC, pick up and k 214 sts evenly along side edge of throw.

Work even in garter st for 8 rows.

Bind off knitwise.

Rep for rem side border.

Top Border

With CC, pick up and k 172 sts evenly along bound-off edge.

Work as for side border.

Rep border along cast-on edge. ●

Chocolate Tweed Throw

Design by Sandi Prosser

A chocolate background and sparkling colors make a throw that is yummy enough to eat.

Skill Level

■■□□ EASY

Finished Size

Approx 38 x 49 inches

Materials

[4] MEDIUM Plymouth Encore 75 percent acrylic/25 percent wool worsted weight yarn (200 yds/100g per skein): 4 skeins chocolate brown #599 (MC), 3 skeins each heather blue #9620 (A) and gold #1014 (B)

- Size 8 (5mm) 29-inch circular needle
- 5-inch piece of cardboard

Gauge

19 sts and 36 rnds = 4 inches/10cm in Tweed pat

To save time, take time to check gauge.

Pattern Stitch

Tweed

Rnds 1 and 2: With MC, knit.

Rnd 3: With A, k1, *sl 1, k1; rep from * around.

Rnd 4: With A, p1, *sl 1 wyib, sl 1 wyif; rep from * around.

Rnds 5 and 6: With B, knit.

Rnd 7: With MC, k2, *sl 1, k1; rep from * to last st, k1.

Rnd 8: With MC, p2, *sl 1 wyib, sl 1 wyif; rep from * to last st, p1.

Rnds 9 and 10: With A, knit.

Rnd 11: With B, k1, *sl 1, k1; rep from * around.

Rnd 12: With B, p1, *sl 1 wyib, sl 1 wyif; rep from * around.

Rnds 13 and 14: With MC, knit.

Rnd 15: With A, k2, *sl 1, k1; rep from * to last st, k1.

Rnd 16: With A, p2, *sl 1 wyib, sl 1 wyif; rep from * to last st, p1.

Rnds 17 and 18: With B, knit.

Rnd 19: With MC, k1, *sl 1, k1; rep from * around.

Rnd 20: With MC, p1, *sl 1 wyib, sl 1 wyif; rep from * around.

Rnds 21 and 22: With A, knit.

Rnd 23: With B, k2, *sl 1, k1; rep from * around.

Rnd 24: With B, p2, *sl 1 wyib, sl 1 wyif; rep from * to last st, p1.

Rep Rnds 1–24 for pat.

Pattern Notes

Afghan is worked in the round with a steek. Steek sts are not included in st counts.

Sl all sts purlwise.

Throw

Cast on 171 sts, pm, cast on 4 sts for steek, pm. Join without twisting.

Work even in Tweed pat until throw measures approx 45 inches, ending with 2 rnds of k sts.

Continued on page 31

rep from * a

Rnd 16: *k
k7; rep from

Rnd 17: *Y
rep from * a

Rnd 18: *Y
p1] twice, LT
around. (84

Rnd 19: *P
times, k7; re

Rnd 20: *Y
times, k1, LT
around. (90

Rnd 21: *Y
3 times, p1,
around. (96

Rnd 22: *k
times, p1, LT
around.

Rnd 23: *Y
times, p1, k
around. (10

Rnd 24: *Y
5 times, k1,

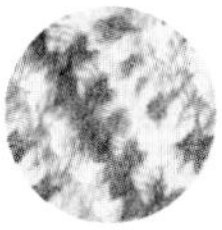

Bind off all

St and cut s

Side Bo

With MC, p
sts evenly a
throw.

Work even
8 rows.

Summer Windows Throw

Design by Nazanin S. Fard

The blocks for this lovely summer throw are worked from the outer edge inward. It's a great travel project.

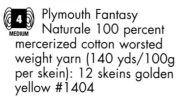

Skill Level

INTERMEDIATE

Finished Size

Approx 44 x 44 inches

Each block measures approx 11 inches

Materials

Plymouth Fantasy Naturale 100 percent mercerized cotton worsted weight yarn (140 yds/100g per skein): 12 skeins golden yellow #1404

- Size 8 (5mm) double-pointed and 29-inch circular needles or size needed to obtain gauge
- Stitch markers
- Size G/6 (4mm) crochet hook
- Tapestry needle

Gauge

16 sts and 24 rnds = 4 inches/10cm in Block pat

To save time, take time to check gauge.

Pattern Notes

Each even-numbered round will be decreased by 8 sts.

The st count listed in parentheses is for 1 side of square only.

Change to dpn when necessary.

Throw

Summer Windows Block

Make 16

Cast on 156 sts. Join without twisting, pm after every 39 sts.

Rnds 1 and 2: Purl.

Rnd 3: Knit.

Rnd 4 and all even-numbered rnds: *Ssk, k to 2 sts before marker, k2tog; rep from * around. (37 sts)

Rnd 5: *K11, yo, ssk, k12, yo, ssk, k10; rep from * around.

Rnd 7: *K8, k2tog, yo, k1, yo, ssk, k9, k2tog, yo, k1, yo, ssk, k8; rep from * around. (35 sts)

Rnd 9: *K6, k2tog, yo, k3, yo, ssk, k7, k2tog, yo, k3, yo, ssk, k6; rep from * around. (33 sts)

Rnd 11: *K4, k2tog, yo, k5, yo, ssk, k5, k2tog, yo, k5, yo, ssk, k4; rep from * around. (31 sts)

Rnd 13: *K5, yo, ssk, k1, k2tog, yo, k9, yo, ssk, k1, k2tog, yo, k5; rep from * around. (29 sts)

Rnd 15: *K5, yo, sl 1, k2tog, psso, yo, k11, yo, sl 1, k2tog, psso, yo, k5; rep from * around. (27 sts)

Rnd 17: *[K5, yo, ssk] 3 times, k4; rep from * around. (25 sts)

Rnd 19: *K9, k2tog, yo, k1, yo, ssk, k9; rep from * around. (23 sts)

Rnd 21: *K7, k2tog, yo, k3, yo, ssk, k7; rep from * around. (21 sts)

Rnd 23: *K5, k2tog, yo, k5,

Continued on page 47

Candlelight Squares

Design by Nazanin S. Fard

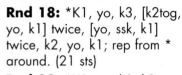

By candlelight or firelight, this afghan will add a glow to any room.

Skill Level

INTERMEDIATE

Finished Size

Approx 48 x 60 inches

Materials

MEDIUM 4 Plymouth Galway 100 percent wool worsted weight yarn (210 yds/100g per skein): 11 skeins lavender #89

- Size 8 (5mm) set of 5 double-pointed and 29-inch circular needles or size needed to obtain gauge
- Size F/5 (3.75mm) crochet hook
- Tapestry needle

Gauge

18 sts and 26 rnds = 4 inches/10cm in Block pat

To save time, take time to check gauge.

Pattern Notes

Each block measures approx 12 inches, and is worked from the center outward.

Numbers in parentheses indicate st count on 1 side of square only.

Change to longer needles when necessary.

Candlelight Block

Make 20

Cast on 12 sts. Divide sts evenly onto 4 needles. Join without twisting, pm between first and last st.

Rnd 1 and all odd-numbered rnds: Knit.

Rnd 2: *[K1, yo] twice, k1; rep from * around. (5 sts)

Rnd 4: *K1, yo, k3, yo, k1; rep from * around. (7 sts)

Rnd 6: *K1, yo, k2tog, yo, k1, yo, ssk, yo, k1; rep from * around. (9 sts)

Rnd 8: *K1, yo, k1, k2tog, yo, k1, yo, ssk, k1, yo, k1; rep from * around. (11 sts)

Rnd 10: *K1, yo, k2, k2tog, yo, k1, yo, ssk, k2, yo, k1; rep from * around. (13 sts)

Rnd 12: *K1, yo, k3, k2tog, yo, k1, yo, ssk, k3, yo, k1; rep from * around. (15 sts)

Rnd 14: *K1, yo, k4, k2tog, yo, k1, yo, ssk, k4, yo, k1; rep from * around. (17 sts)

Rnd 16: *K1, yo, k3, [k2tog, yo] twice, k1, [yo, ssk] twice, k3, yo, k1; rep from * around. (19 sts)

Rnd 18: *K1, yo, k3, [k2tog, yo, k1] twice, [yo, ssk, k1] twice, k2, yo, k1; rep from * around. (21 sts)

Rnd 20: *K1, yo, k3, k2tog, yo, k2, k2tog, yo, k1, yo, ssk, k2, yo, ssk, k3, yo, k1; rep from * around. (23 sts)

Rnd 22: *K1, [yo, k3, k2tog] twice, yo, k1, [yo, ssk, k3] twice, yo, k1; rep from * around. (25 sts)

Rnd 24: *K1, yo, k3, k2tog, yo, k13, yo, ssk, k3, yo, k1; rep from * around. (27 sts)

Rnd 26: *K1, yo, k6, yo, ssk, k9, k2tog, yo, k6, yo, k1; rep from * around. (29 sts)

Rnd 28: *K1, yo, k8, yo, ssk, k7, k2tog, yo, k8, yo, k1; rep from * around. (31 sts)

Rnd 30: *K1, yo, k10, yo, ssk, k5, k2tog, yo, k10, yo, k1; rep from * around. (33 sts)

Rnd 32: *K1, yo, k12, yo, ssk, k3, k2tog, yo, k12, yo, k1; rep from * around. (35 sts)

Rnd 34: *K1, yo, k14, yo, ssk, k1, k2tog, yo, k14, yo, k1; rep from * around. (37 sts)

Rnd 36: *K1, yo, k16, yo, sl 2, k1, p2sso, yo, k16, yo, k1; rep from * around. (39 sts)

Continued on page 47

Dash Stitch Rounds

Design by Sandi Prosser

Slipped strands lie across the front of this throw, giving it an interesting textured effect.

Skill Level

EASY

Finished Size

Approx 40 x 50 inches

Materials

4 MEDIUM Plymouth Galway 100 percent wool worsted weight yarn (210 yds/100g per skein): 8 skeins light kiwi #127 (MC), 3 skeins kiwi #130 (CC)

- Size 7 (4.5mm) 29-inch circular needle or size needed to obtain gauge
- Stitch markers

Gauge

19 sts and 34 rnds = 4 inches/10cm in Dashes pat

To save time, take time to check gauge.

Pattern Stitch

Dashes

Rnds 1, 2, 5 and 6: With MC, knit.

Rnds 3 and 4: With CC, sl 4, *sl 3 wyif, sl 3 wyib; rep from * to last st, sl 1.

Rnds 7 and 8: With CC, sl 1 wyif, sl 3 wyib, *sl 3 wyif, sl 3 wyib; rep from * to last st, sl 1.

Rep Rnds 1–8 for pat.

Pattern Notes

Throw is worked in the round with a steek; keep steek sts in p throughout entire throw.

Steek sts are not included in st counts.

Sl all sts purlwise.

Throw

With MC, cast on 179 sts, pm, cast on 4 sts for steek, pm. Join without twisting.

Work even in Dashes pat until throw measures approx 47 inches, ending with Rnd 2 of pat.

Bind off.

Side Border

With MC, pick up and k 205 sts evenly along side edge of throw.

Work even in garter st for 8 rows.

Bind off knitwise.

Rep for rem side border.

Top Border

With MC, pick up and k 179 sts evenly along bound-off edge.

Work as for side border.

Rep border along cast-on edge. ●

Log Cabin Baby Blanket

Design by Diane Zangl

The traditional quilt pattern Log Cabin inspired this cozy blanket. Soft shades are combined with white to achieve the impression of printed cloth.

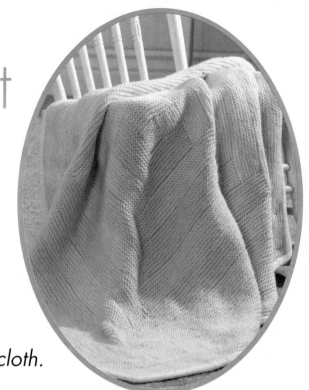

Skill Level

◼◼◻◻
EASY

Size

Approx 40 x 40 inches

Materials

- **3** **LIGHT** Plymouth Dreambaby DK 50 percent nylon/50 percent acrylic DK weight yarn (183 yds/50g per ball): 6 balls each baby pink #119 and white #100, 7 balls baby blue #102
- Size 9 (5.5mm) 29-inch circular needle or size needed to obtain gauge
- Stitch marker

Gauge

16 sts and 32 rows (16 ridges) = 4 inches/10cm in garter st

To save time, take time to check gauge.

Color Sequence

Work 2 blocks each of pink, pink/white, blue, and then blue/white.

Pattern Notes

Two strands of yarn are held tog for entire blanket.

Always give piece a ¼ turn clockwise before picking up sts for next section. With RS facing, pick up sts between ridges along side edge of block and in front strand of bound-off sts.

You will always have a multiple of 8 sts on the needle.

Using a separate strand of yarn to pick up sts for the I-cord edging prevents the unwanted "blip" of another color showing through the edging.

Diagram shows color placement and direction of work for first 3 full rounds of blocks.

Continue with following blocks in same manner.

Blanket

With 2 strands of pink held tog, cast on 8 sts. Knit 15 rows (8 ridges on RS). Mark RS of this square. Bind off, leaving last st on needle.

Give square a ¼ turn clockwise.

Block 2

Cut 1 strand pink, join white. Pick up and k 7 sts along side of first block. Knit 15 rows. Bind off, leaving last st on needle.

Give square a ¼ turn clockwise.

Block 3

Pick up and k 7 sts along side edge of last block, and 8 sts along cast-on edge of Block 1. (16 sts)

Knit 15 rows. Bind off, leaving last st on needle.

Give square a ¼ turn clockwise.

Block 4

Cut yarn, join 2 strands blue. Pick up and k 16 sts along side edge of last block. (16 sts)

Knit 15 rows. Bind off, leaving last st on needle.

Give square a ¼ turn clockwise.

Block 5

Pick up and k 23 sts along side edge of last block. (24 sts)

Knit 15 rows. Bind off, leaving last st on needle.

Give square a ¼ turn clockwise.

Block 6

Cut 1 strand blue, join 1 strand white. Pick up and k 23 sts

along side edge of last block. (24 sts)

Knit 15 rows. Bind off, leaving last st on needle.

Give square a ¼ turn clockwise.

Block 7

Pick up and k 31 sts along side edge of last block. (32 sts)

Knit 15 rows. Bind off, leaving last st on needle.

Give square a ¼ turn clockwise.

Maintaining color sequence, continue to work in this manner, adding a new block onto those previously worked until blanket measures approx 40 inches square.

Bind off all sts of last block (last block will have 160 sts).

I-cord Edging

With 2 strands of white held

tog, pick up and k 1 st in each bound-off stitch of last row.

Drop yarn, do not cut. Return to first picked up st and with separate double strand of white, cast on 4 sts to LH needle.

*K3, ssk (cord st along with picked-up st), sl sts just worked back to LH needle. Rep from * until all picked-up sts have been worked.

Return to first double strand of yarn. Pick up and k along 2nd side of blanket. Continue edging until all picked-up sts along 2nd side have been worked. Rep for rem 2 sides.

Cut yarn and weave final sts to cast-on sts of edging. Hide ends in edging. ●

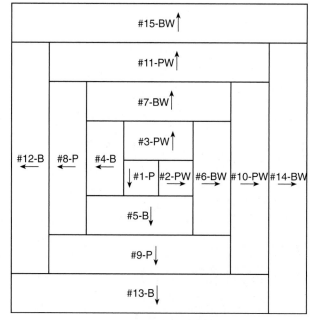

LOG CABIN DIAGRAM

KEY
#1 etc. = Order of work
→ = Direction of work
B = Blue
P = Pink
W = White
BW = Blue & white
PW = Pink & white

Slumber Party Sleeping Bag

Design by Jacqueline Hoyle

Knitting an afghan in the round transforms it into a delightful child's sleeping bag.

Skill Level

INTERMEDIATE

Finished Size

48 (50, 51, 53) x 48 (48, 57, 57) inches Instructions are given for smallest size, with larger sizes in parentheses. When only 1 number is given, it applies to all sizes.

Materials

5 BULKY Plymouth Encore Chunky 75 percent acrylic/25 percent wool chunky weight yarn (143 yds/100g per skein): 8 (8, 9, 9) skeins aqua #235 (A), 3 balls chartreuse #3335 (B)

3 LIGHT Dreambaby Kokonut DK 67 percent microfiber acrylic/33 percent nylon DK weight yarn (126 yds/50g per ball): 1(1, 2, 2) balls white #400 (C)

4 MEDIUM Plymouth Flash 100 percent nylon novelty eyelash yarn (190 yds/50g per ball): 1 ball lavender #965 (D)

- Size 15 (10mm) double-pointed (2 only) and 36-inch circular needles or size needed to obtain gauge
- Stitch marker
- Stitch holder
- Tapestry needle

Gauge

16 sts and 27 rows = 4 inches/10cm in Triple-Slip St pat

15 sts and 16 rows = 4 inches/10cm in Three Flower pat

To save time, take time to check gauge.

Special Abbreviations

CD: Hold 1 strand each of C and D together.

MB (Make Bobble): P3, turn, k3, turn, sl 1, k2tog, psso.

Pattern Stitches

Three Flowers (multiple of 10 sts)

Rnds 1–4: With A, knit.

Rnd 5: With B, knit.

Rnd 6: With B, *p3 wrapping yarn 3 times for each st, p7; rep from * around.

Rnd 7: With A, *sl 3 wyib dropping extra wraps, k3, sl 1 wyib, k3; rep from * around.

Rnd 8: With A, sl 3 wyib, k3, sl 1 wyib, k3; rep from * around.

Rnds 9 and 10: With A, * sl 3 wyib, k7; rep from * around.

Rnd 11: With A, sl 1 B wyib, *k1 B, drop next B st off needle to front of work, k2, place dropped st back on LH needle and knit it, k3, sl 2 wyib, drop next B st off needle to front of work, place 2 sl sts back on LH needle, pick up dropped st and knit it, k2; rep from *, end last rep sl 2 wyib, drop B off

LH needle, sl 2 sts back onto LH needle, place dropped st on LH needle, k3.

Rnd 12: With CD, *(k1, p1, k1) in next st, sl 2 wyib, (k1, p1, k1) in next st, sl 3 wyib, (k1, p1, k1) in next st, sl 2 wyib; rep from *, end last rep (k1, p1, k1) in next st, sl 2 wyib.

Rnd 13: With CD, *MB, sl 2 wyib, MB, sl 3 wyib, *[MB, sl 2 wyib] twice, MB, sl 3 wyib; rep from *, end last rep MB, sl 2 wyib.

Rnd 14: With A, knit, working each bobble tbl.

Rnds 15–18: Rep Rnds 1–4.

Pattern Notes

One strand each of C and D are always held together.

When working in the round, read all rnds from right to left, working area between red lines only.

When working in rows, all uneven-numbered rows are RS rows. Work complete chart, including selvage sts.

To prevent long float on Rnds 10 and 20 of chart, work as follows: wyif, carry yarn across 3 sts at end of row, sl marker, sl first st of new row to RH needle, wyib place same st back on LH needle; wyif sl 3 sts to RH needle and continue in pat across row.

Sleeping Bag

With A, cast on 180 (186, 192, 198) sts. Join without twisting, pm between first and last st.

*[Work Rnds 1–20 of chart] twice.

Work Rnds 1–18 of Three Flowers pat, dec 0 (6, 2, 8) sts on first rnd and inc 0 (6, 2, 8) sts on last rnd.

Rep from * 3 (3, 4, 4) times. Bag will measure approx 41 (41, 51, 51) inches.

Top Flaps

Work in rows from this point.

Row 1: With B, k 90 (93, 96, 99) sts, inc 5 (2, 5, 2) sts evenly. Place rem sts on holder. (95, 95, 101, 101 sts)

Keeping first and last st in St st for selvage, work even from chart until 40 rows have been completed.

Work in garter st for 3 rows, inc (inc, dec, dec) 5 (5, 1, 1) sts on first row. (100 sts)

Knit 1 row, place sts on holder.

Sl st from first holder to needle. Work 2nd flap the same.

Border Triangles
Make 10

With color of your choice, cast on 2 sts.

Next row: *Yo, k to end of row.

Rep this row until there are 20 sts on needle.

Place sts on holder.

Finishing

Place 5 triangles on 1 needle; place sts of 1 top flap on 2nd needle.

Holding needles parallel, k2tog (1 st from each needle) across row.

Bind off.

Rep for 2nd side.

Tack triangles to outside of bag.

I-Cord Trim

With A, cast on 3 sts.

*K3, sl sts back to LH needle; rep from * until cord measures 1½ times the width of bottom of bag. Place sts on holder.

With B, make 2nd cord the same.

Finishing

Twist cords tog loosely and pin to bottom edge of bag, adjusting length of cords if necessary.

Bind off and sew in place. ●

STITCH KEY
☐ K on RS, p on WS
⊟ Sl 1 wyif on RS, sl 1 wyib on WS.

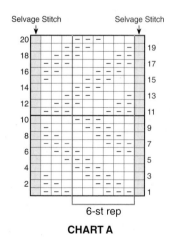

6-st rep

CHART A

Summer Windows Throw
Continued from page 32

yo, ssk, k5; rep from * around. (19 sts)

Rnd 25: *K6, yo, ssk, k1, k2tog, yo, k6; rep from * around. (17 sts)

Rnd 27: *K6, yo, sl 1, k2tog, psso, yo, k6; rep from * around. (15 sts)

Rnd 29: *K6, yo, ssk, k5; rep from * around. (13 sts)

Rnd 31: Knit.

Rnd 33: *K1, [yo, ssk] 4 times; rep from * around. (9 sts)

Rnds 35, 37 and 39: Knit.

Cut yarn leaving a 6-inch end. Draw yarn through rem sts twice and pull tightly.

Weave in ends on WS.

Finishing

Sew 4 blocks tog to form a long strip.

Sew 4 strips tog to form a throw of 4 blocks x 4 blocks.

Edging

Work 1 rnd sc around entire afghan, making sure to keep work flat.

Join with sl st. ●

Candlelight Squares
Continued from page 34

Rnd 38: *K1, yo, k37, yo, k1; rep from * around. (41 sts)

Rnd 40: *K1, yo, p39, yo, k1; rep from * around. (43 sts)

Rnd 42: *K1, yo, p41, yo, k1; rep from * around. (45 sts)

Rnd 43: Knit.

Bind off all sts loosely.

Finishing

Sew blocks tog, having 5 rows of 4 blocks each.

Work 1 rnd of sc around entire afghan, making sure to keep work flat.

Join with sl st. ●

Well-Rounded Kids

There isn't a better way to spend your weekends than knitting for that precious baby or youngster in your life! Use the colors kids love to knit them a sweater or colorful top. Expect hugs and kisses when you give these gifts.

Baby Fluff

Designs by Lainie Hering

A classic baby set, trimmed with chic bands of pastel fluff, is a perfect gift for a special baby.

Skill Level

INTERMEDIATE

Size

Child's 0–3 (6–9, 12–18) months

Instructions are given for smallest size, with larger sizes in parentheses. When only 1 number is given, it applies to all sizes.

Finished Measurements

Sweater chest: 22 (23, 24) inches

Materials

4 MEDIUM Plymouth Encore Worsted 75 percent acrylic/25 percent wool worsted weight yarn (200 yds/100g per skein): 3 skeins off-white #146 (MC)

5 BULKY Plymouth Firenze 40 percent nylon/30 percent wool/30 percent acrylic novelty yarn (55 yds/50g per ball): 1 ball baby #441 (CC)

- Size 6 (4mm) needles
- Size 7 (4.5mm) 16-inch circular needle
- Size 8 (5mm) double-pointed, 16- and 24-inch circular needle or size needed to obtain gauge
- 1 (¾-inch) button

- 1 yd (⅜-inch) off-white double-faced satin ribbon
- Stitch markers
- Stitch holders

Gauge

18 sts and 25 rnds = 4 inches/10cm in St st with MC and size 8 needles

To save time, take time to check gauge.

Special Abbreviation

M1 (Make 1): With LH needle, lift strand between last st worked and next st on LH needle, and knit into back of it.

Pattern Stitches

Seed Stitch (worked in rnds)

Rnd 1: *K1, p1; rep from * around.

Rnd 2: *P1, k1; rep from * around.

Rep Rnds 1–2 for pat.

Seed Stitch (worked in rows)

All rows: *K1, p1; rep from * across.

Stripe Sequence

Knit 3 rnds CC, 4 (5, 5) rnds MC, 3 rnds CC.

Pattern Note

Sweater is worked from the neck downward.

Sweater

Beg at neck with MC and largest needle, cast on 36 sts. Do not join.

Setup row (RS): K1, pm, k1 (seam st), pm, k6 (sleeve), pm, k1 (seam st), pm, k18 (back), pm, k1 (seam st), pm, k6 (sleeve), pm, k1 (seam st), pm, k1.

Purl 1 row.

Beg neck shaping

Inc row 1: *K to marker, M1, sl marker, k seam st, sl marker, M1; rep from * 3 times, k to end of row. (44 sts)

Purl 1 row.

Inc row 2: Continue to inc at markers as before, *at the same time* inc 1 st in each end st by knitting into the front and back of st.

Purl 1 row.

[Rep last 2 rows] 3 times. (84 sts)

Join for yoke

Next row: Rep inc row 1, cast on 8 sts at end of row, join and k to first marker. (100 sts)

Marker between front and right sleeve will now denote beg of rnd.

Beg stripe

Beg stripe pat when there are 32 (34, 34) sts on front, *at the same time* continue to inc at

markers [every other rnd] 3 (5, 6) times, then [every 4th rnd] once. (132, 148, 156 sts)

Work even until yoke measures 5 (5½, 6) inches when measured at center back.

Divide work

Sl sts onto 4 separate holders as follows: 26 (30, 32) sts for each sleeve, 38 (42, 44) back or front sts plus 2 seam sts.

Sleeves

Next rnd: With size 8 dpn, cast on 4 sts, k 26 (30, 32) sleeve sts from holder, cast on 4 sts, divide sts among dpn, pm between first and last st. (34, 38, 40 sts)

Working in St st, [dec 1 st each side of marker every 8th (6th, 7th) rnd] 3 (4, 4) times. (28, 30, 32 sts)

Work even until sleeve measures 4½ (5, 5½) inches.

Knit 3 rnds in CC.

Change to MC and work even until sleeve measures 6 (6½, 7) inches.

Bind off.

Body

Sl front and back sts from holders to size 8 circular needle. Mark this rnd.

Cast on 4 sts, k front sts, cast on 4 sts, pm, cast on 4 sts, k back sts, cast on 4 sts, pm to denote beg of rnd.

Work even until body measures 4½ (5½, 6) inches above marker.

Change to size 7 needles.

Work even in Seed St for 1 inch.

Bind off in pat.

Neck Band

With MC and size 7 needle, pick up and k 60 sts around neck edge.

Work even in Seed St for ¾ (1, 1) inch.

Bind off in pat.

Sew underarm seam, using Kitchener st.

Hat

With MC and size 7 needle, cast on 57 (61, 65) sts.

Work in Seed St for 1 inch. Change to size 8 needle.

With CC, work 4 rows St st. Cut CC, join MC.

Work even until hat measures 4½ (5, 5½) inches, ending with a WS row.

[Dec 1 st each end every row] 6 times. (45, 49, 53 sts)

Bind off 5 sts at beg of next 4 rows.

Bind off rem 25 (29, 33) sts.

Fold hood in half and sew back seam.

Neck Band

With RS facing and size 7 needle pick up and k 38 (40, 44) sts evenly around lower edge of hat, cast on 11 (11, 13) sts. (49, 51, 57 sts)

Work even in k1, p1 rib for 7 rows making buttonhole on Row 4.

Buttonhole row (RS): Work in pat to last 4 sts, yo, k2tog, p1, k1.

Bind off in pat.

Finishing

Sew on button.

Make a small pompom using 1 strand each of MC and CC held tog.

Sew pompom to point of hat.

Booties

With CC and size 6 needle, cast on 32 sts.

Knit 1 row, purl 1 row. Change to MC.

Work even in k2, p2 rib for 8 (8, 10) rows.

Eyelet row: K1, *yo, k2tog; rep from * across, end last rep k1.

Next row: P14, pm, p4, pm, p14.

Inc row: K to 1 st before marker, M1, k1, k to next marker, k1, M1, k to end of row.

Purl 1 row.

[Rep last 2 rows] 5 (6, 6) times. (44, 46, 46 sts)

Size 12–18 months only:
Knit 1 row, purl 1 row.

All sizes: Work even in garter st for 8 (9, 10) rows.

Bind off.

Finishing

Sew sole and back of bootie.

Cut ribbon to measure 18 inches and weave through eyelet row. ●

Cuddly Baby Bunting

Design by Kennita Tully

Baby will be both stylish and toasty in a bunting with attached hood.

Skill Level

INTERMEDIATE

Size

Infant's 0–3 (3–6, 6–9, 9–12) months

Instructions are given for smallest size, with larger sizes in parentheses. When only 1 number is given, it applies to all sizes.

Finished Measurements

Chest: 22 (24, 25½, 27) inches

Length: 22 (23, 24, 25) inches

Materials

1 SUPER FINE Plymouth Forever Jacquard 75 percent wool/25 percent polyamide sock yarn (230 yds/50g per ball): 3 (3, 4, 4) balls sea blues #80

- Size 2 (2.75mm) double-pointed and 16-inch circular needles
- Size 3 (3.25mm) double-pointed, 16- and 24-inch circular needles or size needed to obtain gauge

- Stitch markers
- Stitch holders
- Tapestry needle
- 4 (5, 5, 6) hook-and-loop tape dots

Gauge

27 sts and 32 rows = 4 inches/10cm in St st with larger needles

To save time, take time to check gauge.

Body

Hem
Make 2

With smaller 16-inch circular needle, cast on 75 (81, 87, 91) sts.

Work even in St st for ¾ inch. Change to larger needles and work even for ¾ inch more.

With smaller needles, pick up each cast-on st. Fold hem in half, having WS tog.

Next row (RS): With needles held parallel, insert RH needle in first st of front and back needles, k2tog. Continue joining sts of both needles, by working k2tog to end of row.

Place sts on holder. Make 2nd hem, leave sts on needle.

Join for body

K across sts on holder, pm, k to end of rnd. Join, pm between first and last st. (150, 162, 174, 182 sts)

Work even in St st until body measures 16½ (17, 17½, 18) inches.

Place all sts on holder.

Sleeves

With smaller dpn, cast on 38 (38, 42, 44) sts.

Knit 6 rnds, change to larger needles and knit 6 more rnds.

Fold hem in half and join as for body.

Next rnd: Knit, inc 4 sts evenly. (42, 42, 46, 48 sts)

Knit 3 rnds.

[Inc 1 st each side of marker every 4th rnd] 3 (9, 5, 6) times, then [every 6th (0, 6th, 6th] rnd 4 (0, 4, 4) times. (56, 60, 64, 68 sts)

Work even until sleeve measures 5 (5½, 6, 6½) inches.

Knit 1 rnd, ending 6 (6, 7, 7) sts before marker.

Place 12 (12, 14, 14) sts on holder, place rem sts on 2nd holder.

Yoke

Joining sleeves and body

K 63 (69, 73, 77) sts for front, place next 12 (12, 14, 14) sts on holder for underarm, k 44 (48, 50, 54) sts for right sleeve, k 63 (69, 73, 77) sts for back, place next 12 (12, 14, 14) sts on holder for under-arm, k 44 (48, 50, 54) sleeve sts. Pm between first and last st. (214, 234, 246, 262 sts)

Mark joining rnd.

Work even until yoke measures 2¾ (3, 3¼, 3½) inches above marker.

Dec rnd: *K1, k2tog; rep from * around. (144, 156, 164, 176 sts)

Work even until yoke measures 4¼ (4½, 4¾, 5) inches above marker.

Rep dec rnd. (96, 104, 112, 120 sts)

Work even until yoke measures 5½ (6, 6½, 7) inches above marker

Rep dec rnd. (64, 72, 76, 80 sts)

Hood

Removing previous markers, mark center front.

K to marker st, turn, purl to end of rnd.

Work in rows from this point.

Next row (RS): Knit, inc 13 (11, 13, 15) sts. (77, 83, 89, 95 sts)

Work even in St st until hood measures 6 inches, ending with a RS row.

Next row: P38 (41, 44, 47), purl next st and mark it, p to end of row.

Shape back

[K to 2 sts before marked st, ssk, k1, k2tog. Purl 1 row] 4 times. (69, 75, 81, 87 sts)

Next row (WS): Dec 1 st at center of hood.

Finishing

Fold hood in half and join top seam using Kitchener st.

Sew underarm seam in same manner.

Sew 4 (5, 5, 6) hook-and-loop tape buttons to bottom hem of bunting. ●

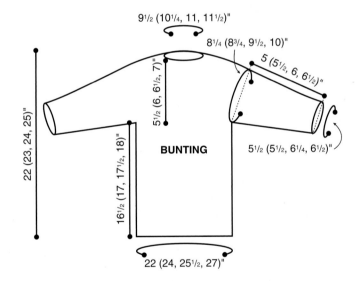

9½ (10¼, 11, 11½)"

8¼ (8¾, 9½, 10)"

5 (5½, 6, 6½)"

5½ (6, 6½, 7)"

22 (23, 24, 25)"

16½ (17, 17½, 18)"

BUNTING

5½ (5½, 6¼, 6½)"

22 (24, 25½, 27)"

Houndstooth Toddler Set

Designs by Lois S. Young

Sophisticated houndstooth checks highlight a toddler's jacket and hat.

Skill Level

◼◼◼▢
INTERMEDIATE

Size

Infant's or Toddler's 6 (12, 18, 24) months

Instructions are given for smallest size, with larger sizes in parentheses. When only 1 number is given, it applies to all sizes.

Finished Measurements

Hat Circumference: 16 (16, 16½, 17) inches

Chest (buttoned): 22 (22½, 23½, 24½) inches

Length: 11¼ (12, 12¾, 14) inches

Materials

Plymouth Wildflower D.K. 51 percent cotton/49 percent acrylic DK weight yarn (136yards/50g per balls): 3 (3, 4, 4) balls medium denim #10 (MC), 2 (2, 3, 3) balls silver gray #30 (CC)

- Size 4 (3.5mm) double-pointed, 16- and 24-inch circular needles or size needed to obtain gauge
- Stitch markers
- Stitch holders
- 5 (7, 7, 7) ½-inch buttons

Gauge

24 sts and 29 rows = 4 inches/10cm in Houndstooth pat

To save time, take time to check gauge.

Special Abbreviations

CDD (Centered Double Decrease): Slip 2 sts as if to k2tog, k1 CC, pass 2 slipped sts over k st.

M1 (Make 1): Make a backward loop and place on RH needle.

Pattern Notes

On hat, change to dpn when necessary.

Cardigan is worked back and forth in rows; do not join.

When working front bands, buttonhole band is placed on right for girls and on left for boys.

Hat

With MC and shorter circular needle, cast on 90 (90, 100, 110) sts, pm every 18 (18, 20, 22) sts. Join without twisting, pm between first and last st.

Referring to Chart A, beg and end as indicated for chosen size, *k 17 (19, 19, 21) in color pat, k 1 MC; rep from * around.

Work even in established pat until hat measures 2½ (3, 3, 3½) inches.

Shape crown

Dec rnd: *Work in established pattern to 1 st before marker, sl 1, remove marker, replace sl st to LH needle,

CDD, replace marker; rep from * around.

Knit one rnd.

Rep last 2 rnds until there are 10 (12, 12, 14) sts between markers, then rep dec rnd every rnd until 10 sts rem.

Next rnd: With CC, ssk around.

Cut yarn, leaving a 12-inch end. Draw through rem sts twice and fasten off.

Brim

With MC and shorter circular needle, pick up and k 92 (92, 100, 108) sts along cast-on edge of hat. Join, pm between first and last st.

Purl 1 rnd.

Next rnd: *M1, k4; rep from * around. (115, 115, 125, 135 sts)

Rnd 2: Purl.

Rnd 3: *M1, k5; rep from * around. (136, 136, 150, 162 sts)

Rnd 4: Purl.

Continue to inc every other rnd, having 1 more st between incs on each rnd until there are

4 (5, 5, 6) ridges on brim.

Knit 1 rnd.

Bind off purlwise.

Cardigan

Body

With MC and longer circular needle, cast on 126 (130, 134, 142) sts.

Knit 7 rows.

Referring to Chart B, work even in Houndstooth pat until body measures 7 (7½, 8, 8½) inches, ending with a WS row.

Divide for fronts and back

K 25 (26, 27, 29) sts and place on holder for right front, bind off 12 sts for underarm, k 52 (54, 56, 60) sts for back and place on 2nd holder, bind off 12 sts for underarm, K 25 (26, 27, 29) sts for left front.

Left Front

Working in established pat, [dec 1 st at arm edge every other row] 3 times. (22, 23, 24, 26 sts)

Work even until armhole measures 3¼ (3½, 3¾, 4¼) inches, ending with a RS row.

Shape neck

Bind off 5 (6, 6, 7) sts at beg of next row.

[Dec 1 st at neck edge every other row] twice. (15, 15, 16, 17 sts)

Work even until armhole measures 4¼ (4½, 4¾, 5½) inches, ending with a WS row.

Bind off shoulder sts with MC.

Right Front

Sl sts from holder to needle. With WS facing, join yarns at underarm.

Work as for left front, reversing shaping.

Back

With WS facing, join yarns at armhole.

[Dec 1 st each end every other row] 3 times. (46, 48, 50, 54 sts)

Work even until armhole measures same as for front.

Next row (RS): With MC only, bind off 15 (15, 16, 17) sts for right shoulder, k next 16 (18, 18, 20) sts and put on holder for back neck, bind off 15 (15, 16, 17) sts for left shoulder.

Sleeves

With MC and shorter circular needle, cast on 44 (46, 48, 52) sts.

Knit 6 rows, inc 6 sts evenly on last row. (50, 52, 54, 58 sts)

Referring to Chart B, work even until sleeve measures 7 (8, 9, 10) inches, ending with a WS row.

[Dec 1 st each end every other row] 3 times.

Bind off rem 44 (46, 48, 52) sts. Sew shoulder seams.

Collar

With RS facing using MC and shorter circular needle, k across 5 (6, 6, 7) sts of right front neck, pick up and k 5 (6, 8, 10) sts along right neck edge, k 16 (18, 18, 20) sts of back neck, pick up and k 5 (6, 8, 10) sts along left neck edge, k 5 (6, 6, 7) sts of left front neck. (36, 42, 46, 54 sts)

Row 1: Sl 1 purlwise, M1, k to last st, M1, k1.

Row 2: Sl 1 purlwise, k to end of row.

[Rep Rows 1 and 2] 3 times. Bind off purlwise.

Button Band

With RS facing using MC and shorter circular needle, pick up and k 3 sts for every 4 rows along front edge.

Knit 6 rows.

Bind off.

Buttonhole Band

Pick up and k as for button band.

Knit 3 rows. Mark front edge for 5 (7, 7, 7) buttonholes evenly spaced.

Buttonhole row: [K to marker, k2tog, yo] 5 (7, 7, 7) times, k to end of row.

Knit 2 rows.

Bind off.

Finishing

Sew sleeve into armhole, having top 1 inch of sleeve edge across bound-off underarm sts.

Sew sleeve seams. ●

COLOR KEY
■ Medium denim (MC)
□ Silver gray (CC)

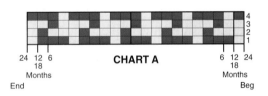

CHART A

24 12 6 18 Months End

6 12 24 18 Months Beg

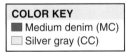
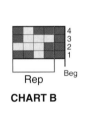

4 3 2 1 Beg

Rep

CHART B

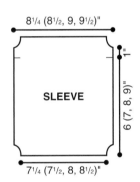

8¼ (8½, 9, 9½)"

1"

SLEEVE

6 (7, 8, 9)"

7¼ (7½, 8, 8½)"

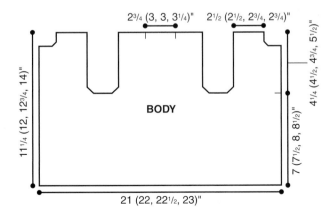

2¾ (3, 3, 3¼)"   2½ (2½, 2¾, 2¾)"

11¼ (12, 12¾, 14)"

BODY

4¼ (4½, 4¾, 5½)"

7 (7½, 8, 8½)"

21 (22, 22½, 23)"

Cast on 3 sts, knit across front sts, cast on 3 sts.

Work as for back until sleeve measures 2½ (2½, 3) inches, ending with a WS row.

Shape neck

Next row (RS): K31 (32, 33), join 2nd ball of yarn and bind off next 10 (12, 12) sts, k to end of row.

Working on both sides of neck with separate balls of yarn, [bind off 2 sts each side of neck] 3 times. (25, 26, 27 sts on each side of neck)

Work even until sleeve measures same as for back.

Bind off rem sts.

Sew shoulder seams.

Neck Band

With D and RS facing, pick up and k 61 (65, 67) sts around neck. Work even in k1, p1 rib for ¾ inch.

Bind off in ribbing.

Sleeve Band

With C, pick up and k 56 (56, 60) sts around lower edge of sleeve.

Work even in k1, p1 ribbing for ¾ (¾, 1) inch.

Bind off in ribbing.

Finishing

Attach D at top corner of left back. With crochet hook, ch 6, join to center st of neck band. Fasten off.

Make a second lp about 1 inch below first lp, using color to match adjoining stripe.

Sew underarm seam.

Sew on buttons. ●

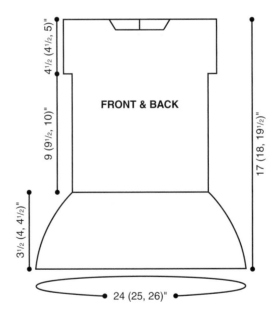

4½ (4½, 5)"

9 (9½, 10)"

FRONT & BACK

17 (18, 19½)"

3½ (4, 4½)"

24 (25, 26)"

Angel Baby

Design by Barbara Venishnick

Citrus and confetti-like colors combine in a dress fit for an angel.

Skill Level

EASY

Size

Child's 2 (4, 6, 8) Instructions are given for smallest size, with larger sizes in parentheses. When only 1 number is given, it applies to all sizes.

Finished Measurements

Chest: 23 (25, 27, 29) inches

Length: 15¾ (17¾, 19¾, 21¾) inches

Materials

3 **LIGHT** Plymouth Dreambaby Kokonut D.K. 67 percent acrylic/33 percent nylon DK weight yarn (126 yds/50g per ball): 3 (4, 5, 6) balls banana #504 (MC)

4 **MEDIUM** Plymouth Flash 100 percent nylon novelty eyelash yarn (190 yds/50g per ball): 1 ball lime #970 (CC)

- Size 6 (4mm) 16-, 24- and 29-inch circular needles or size needed to obtain gauge
- Size D/3 crochet hook
- Stitch markers

Gauge

20 sts and 30 rnds = 4 inches/10cm with MC in St st

To save time, take time to check gauge.

Dress

With longest needle and MC, cast on 160 (172, 184, 196) sts. Join without twisting, pm between first and last st.

Work even in St st for 1½ inches.

Purl 1 rnd for turning rnd.

Change to CC and knit 1 rnd.

Work even in rev St st for 1½ inches. Change to MC and knit 1 rnd, pm after every 40th (43rd, 46th, 49th) st.

Dec rnd: [K to marker, k2tog] 4 times.

Knit 4 (5, 5, 6) rnds.

[Rep these 5 (6, 6, 7) rnds] 11 times, changing to shorter needles when necessary. (112, 124, 136, 148 sts)

Work even until dress measures 10 (11½, 13, 14½) inches above turning rnd.

Divide work

Place last 56 (62, 68, 74) sts worked on holder for front.

Work in rows from this point.

Back

Bind off 3 sts at beg of the next 2 rows, then 2 sts at beg of following 2 rows.

[Dec 1 st each end every other row] 3 times. (40, 46, 52, 58 sts)

Work even until armhole measures 5 (5½, 6, 6½) inches, ending with a WS row.

Shape neck and shoulders

Next row (RS): K13 (15, 17, 19), join 2nd ball of yarn and bind off center 14 (16, 18, 20) sts, k13 (15, 17, 19). Working on both sides of neck with separate balls of yarn, [dec 1 st at each neck edge every other row] 3 times, *at the same time* bind off at each arm edge 3 (4, 5, 5) sts twice, then 4 (4, 4, 6) sts once.

Front

Work as for back until armhole measures 2½ (3, 3½, 4) inches, ending with a WS row.

Shape neck

Next row (RS): K13 (15, 17, 19), join 2nd ball of yarn and bind off center 14 (16, 18, 20) sts, k13 (15, 17, 19).

[Dec 1 st at each side of neck every other row] 3 times. (10, 12, 14, 16 sts)

Work even until armhole measures same as for back.

Shape shoulders

Bind off at each arm edge 3 (4, 5, 5) sts twice, then 4 (4, 4, 6) sts once.

Sew shoulder seams.

Neck Band

Beg at right shoulder with RS facing using shortest needle and CC, pick up and k 8 sts along right neck edge, 14 (16, 18, 20) sts of back neck, 25 sts along left neck, 14 (16, 18, 20) sts of front neck, and 17 sts along right neck edge. Pm between first and last st. 78 (82, 86, 90 sts)

Work even in St st for 1½ inches.

Bind off very loosely, using a larger needle if desired.

Armhole Edging

With MC, work 1 rnd sc around entire armhole, making sure to keep work flat. Join with sl st, do not turn.

Working from left to right, work 1 sc in each sc of previous rnd.

Join with sl st, fasten off.

Rep around rem armhole. ●

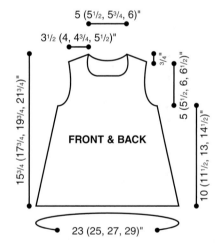

5 (5½, 5¾, 6)"

3½ (4, 4¾, 5½)"

¾"

5 (5½, 6, 6½)"

15¾ (17¾, 19¾, 21¾)"

FRONT & BACK

10 (11½, 13, 14½)"

23 (25, 27, 29)"

Polar Jacket

Design by Diane Zangl

Traditional Northwest Coast styling and nontraditional colors combine in the Polar Jacket, which features a hood to keep small ears warm and raglan sleeves to allow for growth.

Skill Level

Size

Child's 6 (8, 10, 12)

Instructions are given for smallest size, with larger sizes in parentheses. When only 1 number is given, it applies to all sizes.

Finished Measurements

Chest: 28 (30, 32, 34) inches
Armhole depth: 7 (7½, 8, 8½) inches
Side to underarm: 9½ (10, 11, 12) inches
Sleeve length: 13 (14, 16, 17) inches

Materials

5 BULKY Plymouth Yukon 35 percent mohair/35 percent wool/30 percent acrylic bulky weight yarn (60 yds/100g per skein): 7 (8, 10, 12) skeins ice blue #85 (MC), 1 skein each red #54 (A) and white #70 (B)

- Size 8 (5mm) 29-inch circular needle
- Size 9 (5.5mm) 29-inch circular needle or size needed to obtain gauge
- Stitch markers
- Stitch holders
- Size J/10 (6mm) crochet hook
- 14- (16-, 16-, 18-) inch separating zipper

Gauge

12 sts and 17 rows = 4 inches/10cm in St st with larger needles

To save time, take time to check gauge.

Pattern Stitch

Raglan Dec Row (RS): [K to 2 sts before marker, k2tog, sl marker, ssk] 4 times, k to end of row.

Pattern Notes

Sleeves may be worked first and used as gauge swatch.

Circular needle is used to accommodate large number of sts. Do not join; work in rows.

Color pats are worked using Fair Isle method. White portions of snowflake pat are worked as duplicate st after garment is completed.

Body

With MC and smaller needle, cast on 81 (87, 93, 99) sts. Work even in k1, p1 ribbing for 1 (1½, 1½, 1½) inches, inc 4 sts on last WS row. (85, 91, 97, 103 sts)

Change to larger needle and St st. Work even for 2 (4, 4, 6) rows.

Referring to Chart A, beg border pat on next RS row.

When chart is completed, work even with MC only until body measures 9½ (10, 11, 12) inches, ending with a WS row.

Divide for fronts and back

K 18 (20, 20, 23) sts, bind off next 6 (6, 8, 10) sts for right

underarm, k 37 (39, 41, 41) sts for back, bind off next 6 (6, 8, 10) sts for left underarm, k to end of row. Do not cut yarn. Place sts on holder and set aside.

Sleeves

With smaller needles and MC, cast on 19 (19, 25, 31) sts. Work even in k1, p1 rib until cuff measures 2 inches, changing to larger needles on last WS row.

Change to St st and [inc 1 st at each end every 4th (4th, 6th, 6th) row] 7 (9, 7, 6) times, *at the same time,* beg border pat of Chart A on 3rd (5th, 5th 7th) row. (33, 37, 39, 43 sts)

Work even until sleeve measures 13 (14, 16, 17) inches, ending with a WS row.

Next row: Bind off 3 (3, 4, 5) sts, k 27 (31, 31, 33) sts, bind off last 3 (3, 4, 5) sts.

Cut yarn and sl sts to holder.

Yoke

With WS facing and pm between each section, purl across sts of left front, sleeve, back, 2nd sleeve, and right front. Mark this row.

[Work Raglan Dec Row every 4th row] 2 (2, 3, 5) times, then [every other row] 9 (10, 9, 6) times, *at the same time,* beg Snowflake pat from Chart B on 3rd (5th, 5th, 8th) row. Flakes beg 1 st in from each front edge and are centered on back and sleeves.

When yoke measures 4½ (5, 5, 5½) inches above marker, beg neck shaping.

Shape neckline

Bind off 4 (5, 5, 6) sts at beg of next 2 rows.

[Dec 1 st at each neck edge every row] 2 (2, 2, 5) times.

Work even at neck edge and continue until raglan decs are complete.

Size 12 only: Work 1 more row, dec 2 sts in each sleeve.

You will have 1 st for each front, 5 (7, 7, 9) sts for each sleeve and 15 (15, 17, 19) sts for back neck. Cut yarn, leave sts on needle.

Hood

With RS facing, using MC and RH needle, pick up and k 7 (8, 8, 10) sts along right neck edge, k across 27 (31, 33, 39) sts left on needle, pick up and k 7 (8, 8, 10) sts along left neck edge. (41, 47, 49, 59 sts)

Mark center st and keep it in rev St st for entire hood.

Working rem sts in St st, [inc 1 st each side of marked st every 6th row] 3 (3, 4, 4) times. (47, 53, 57, 67 sts)

Work even until hood measures 11 (12, 13, 14) inches. Do not bind off.

Fold hood in half and join top seam using Kitchener st.

Finishing

Join MC at lower right front edge. Work 1 row sc up right front, around entire hood, and down left front, making sure to keep work flat. Do not turn.

Row 2: Working from left to right, work 1 sc in each sc of previous row.

Fasten off.

Sew sleeve and underarm seams.

Duplicate st white sts on snowflakes.

Sew in zipper. ●

COLOR KEY

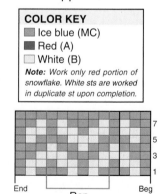

- ▦ Ice blue (MC)
- ■ Red (A)
- □ White (B)

Note: Work only red portion of snowflake. White sts are worked in duplicate st upon completion.

CHART A

CHART B

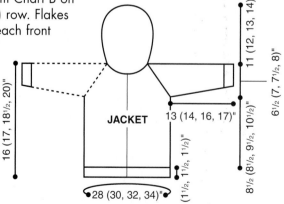

JACKET

16 (17, 18½, 20)"

13 (14, 16, 17)"

8½ (8½, 9½, 10½)"

6½ (7, 7½, 8)"

11 (12, 13, 14)"

1 (1½, 1½, 1½)"

28 (30, 32, 34)"

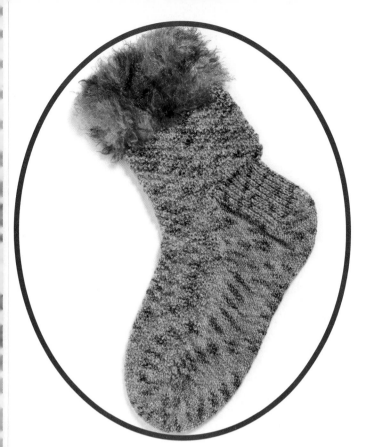

A Little Fluff

Design by Janet Rehfeldt

Fluffy yarn with a bit of sparkle turns ordinary socks into extraordinary accessories.

Skill Level

INTERMEDIATE

Size

Child's 4 (6, 8, 10, 12) Adult [small, medium, large] Instructions are given for smallest size, with larger sizes in parentheses or brackets. When only 1 number is given, it applies to all sizes.

Finished Measurements

Foot Circumference (unstretched): 5½ (6¼, 6¾, 7¼, 8) [8½, 9, 9¾] inches

Materials

1 **SUPER FINE** Plymouth Sockotta 45 percent cotton/40 percent superwash wool/15 percent nylon sock weight yarn (414 yds/100g per skein): 1 (1, 1, 1, 1) [2, 2, 2] skeins circus #16 (MC)

4 **MEDIUM** Plymouth Adriafil Stars 50 percent rayon/50 percent nylon novelty eyelash yarn (71 yds/50g per ball): 1 ball fiesta #48 (CC)

- Size 2 (2.75mm) set of 4 double-pointed needles or size needed to obtain gauge
- Size 4 (3.5mm) set of 4 double-pointed needles
- Stitch marker

Gauge

8½ sts and 12 rnds = 1 inch/ 2.5cm in St st with smaller needles

To save time, take time to check gauge.

Pattern Notes

Hold 1 strand each of MC and CC tog for cuff.

When working with eyelash yarn, you will need to release the fibers on occasion as you knit the cuff. Gently use the tip of the needle to "brush" the eyelash from the stitches. You may also find that you have to release the eyelash from the stitch just before you work it.

Cuff can be folded down for short anklet look.

Choose sock size that is ½–¾ inch narrower than foot circumference.

Sock

Cuff

With 1 strand each of MC and CC held tog and larger needles, cast on 32 (36, 40, 48, 48) [52, 56, 64] sts.

Divide sts onto three needles as follows: 8-16-8 (9-18-9, 10-20-10, 12-24-12, 12-24-12) [13-26-13, 14-28-14, 16-32-16]. Join without twisting, pm between first and last st.

Work even in k2, p2 rib for 1¾ inches.

Knit 1 rnd, cut CC, change to smaller needles.

Next rnd: Knit, inc 4 (4, 4, 4, 5) [5, 5, 5] sts on each of needles #1 and #3, and 8 (8, 8, 8, 10) [10, 10, 10] sts on needle #2. (48, 52, 56, 64, 68) [72, 76, 84 sts]

Silly Hat

Design by Carol May

This warm and colorful topper will bring a smile to any child's face.

Skill Level

■■□□
EASY

Size

Child's medium

Finished Measurements

Circumference: 16 inches

Length without tassel: 22 inches

Materials

4 MEDIUM Plymouth Encore Worsted 75 percent acrylic/25 percent wool worsted weight yarn (200 yds/100g per ball): 1 ball each purple #1033 (A), aqua #1201 (B), tan #240 (C), burgundy #999 (D), light rose #9408 (E) and blue/green multi #7121 (F)

- Size 6 (4mm) double-pointed needles
- Size 7 (4.5mm) double-pointed needles or size needed to obtain gauge
- Stitch marker
- Tapestry needle
- 5-inch-wide piece of stiff cardboard
- Size H/8 (5mm) crochet hook

Gauge

26 sts and 34 rnds = 4 inches/10cm in Broken Stripes pat with larger needles

To save time, take time to check gauge.

Pattern Stitches

Broken Stripes

Rnds 1 and 2: *K3, sl 1; rep from * around.

Rnds 3 and 4: K1, *sl 1, k3; rep from * around.

Rep Rnds 1–4 for pat.

Work in color sequence of 2 rnds each of: E, C, A, F, B, D, C, F, B, E, D, A.

Pattern Note

Carry colors not in use up work.

Hat

With A and smaller needles, cast on 120 sts.

Join without twisting, pm between first and last st.

Work even in k2, p2 rib for 4 inches.

Next rnd: Knit, dec 16 sts evenly. (104 sts)

Change to larger needles and E. Work even in Broken Stripes pat and color sequence until hat measures 4 inches above ribbing.

Beg shaping

Dec rnd: K2tog, work to last 2 sts, ssk.

Work even for 3 rnds.

Working in established pat, rep these 4 rnds until 18 sts rem.

Next rnd: *K2tog; rep from * around. (9 sts)

Cut yarn and draw through rem sts twice.

Tassel

Cut a 16-inch length of A and set aside. Wrap A around cardboard approx 25 times. Tie 1 end with reserved length of yarn. Cut opposite end.

With another 16-inch length of A, wrap around tassel 3 times about 1 inch below first tie. Tie tightly and pull long ends into tassel to hide. Trim tassel even.

With crochet hook using 2 strands of first knot, ch 3, fasten off.

Sew tassel to end of hat, weaving loose ends into inside. ●

Back to School

Designs by Linda K. Roper

Your fashion doll will look fantastic on the first day of school in a matching three-piece set.

Skill Level

EASY

Size

To fit an 11½-inch fashion doll

Materials

1 SUPER FINE Plymouth Gjestal Reggio 80 percent superwash wool/20 percent nylon sock yarn (164 yds/50g per ball): 1 ball jacquard effect #719 (MC)

1 SUPER FINE Plymouth Gjestal Silja 80 percent wool/20 percent nylon sock yarn (164 yds/50g per ball): 1 ball pink #323 (CC)

- Size 3 (3.25mm) double-pointed needles or size needed to obtain gauge
- Stitch markers
- Stitch holders

Gauge

6½ sts and 9 rows = 1 inch/ 2.5cm in St st

To save time, take time to check gauge.

Pattern Note

Neckline is wide enough to fit over doll's torso; ribbing allows stitches to bounce back to shape. Always dress a doll from the feet up, never over the head.

Sweater

Yoke

With MC, cast on 30 sts, divide sts equally on 3 needles. Join without twisting, pm between first and last st.

Rnds 1 and 2: *K1, p1; rep from * around.

Rnd 3: K5, pm, k1, [inc 1 st in next st] twice, k1, pm, k12, pm, k1, [inc 1 st in next st] twice, k1, pm, k5. (34 sts)

Rnd 4: Knit, inc 1 st before and after each marker. (42 sts)

Rnd 5: Knit.

Rnds 6–13: Rep rnds 4 and 5. (74 sts)

Divide for sleeves

Next rnd: Removing markers, k10 for right back, place next 16 sts on holder for sleeve, k 22 sts for front, place 16 sts on 2nd holder for 2nd sleeve, k10 for left back. (42 sts)

Body

Knit 8 rnds, work in k1, p1 ribbing for 2 rnds.

Bind off in ribbing.

Sleeves

Sl sts of 1 sleeve to dpn, having 5 sts on each of first 2 needles, and 6 sts on 3rd needle.

Knit 8 rnds.

Rnd 9: K2tog, k12, k2tog. (14 sts)

Knit 3 rnds.

Work in k1, p1 ribbing for 2 rnds.

Bind off in ribbing.

Work 2nd sleeve as for first.

Skirt

Beg at waist with CC, cast on 26 sts. Divide sts onto 3 needles, having 8 sts on first needle and 9 sts on each of next 2 needles. Join without twisting, pm between first and last st.

Rnds 1–3: *K1, p1; rep from * around.

Rnd 4: Knit.

Rnd 5: [K3, inc 1 st in next st] twice, k10, [inc 1 st in next st, k3] twice. (30 sts)

Rnd 6: Knit.

Rnd 7: [K4, inc 1 st in next st] twice, k10, [inc 1 st in next st, k4] twice. (34 sts)

Work even until skirt measures 3 inches, or desired length.

Next rnd: Purl.

Bind off knitwise.

Hat

With CC, cast on 26 sts. Divide sts onto 3 needles, having 8 sts on first needle and 9 sts on each of next 2 needles. Join without twisting, pm between first and last st.

Rnd 1: Purl.

Rnds 2–7: Knit.

Rnd 8: *K3, k2tog; rep from * to last st, k1. (21 sts)

Rnd 9: Knit.

Rnd 10: *K2 , k2tog; rep from * to last st, k1. (16 sts)

Rnd 11: Knit.

Rnd 12: K1, k2tog; rep from * to last st, k1. (11 sts)

Cut yarn, leaving a 12-inch end. Draw yarn through rem sts twice and pull tightly.

Pull yarn to WS. ●

Party Pants & Bag

Designs by Lynda K. Roper

Let the party begin!
This stylish pants and bag
set will dress any fashion doll in style.

Skill Level

Size

To fit an 11½-inch fashion doll

Materials

1 **SUPER FINE** Plymouth Sockotta 45 percent cotton/40 percent wool/15 percent nylon sock yarn (414 yds/100g per ball): 1 ball blue/green multi #21

- Size 2 (2.75mm) double-pointed needles or size needed to obtain gauge
- Stitch holder

Gauge

7 sts and 10 rnds = 1 inch/2.5cm in St st

To save time, take time to check gauge.

Pants

Beg at top, cast on 44 sts.

Divide onto 3 needles, having 14 sts on first needle and 15 sts on each of next 2 needles. Join without twisting, pm between first and last st.

Rnd 1: *K2, p2, rep from * around.

Begin bib

Row 2: Rib 13 sts, turn.

Row 3: Sl 1, rib 11 sts, turn.

Row 4: Sl 1, rib 10 sts, turn.

Row 5: Sl 1, rib 9 sts, turn.

Row 6: Sl 1, rib 7 sts, turn.

Row 7: Sl 1, rib 5 sts, turn.

Rnd 8: Sl 1, work in established rib to end of rnd.

Work even in rib pat until back measures 1¼ inch.

Shape waist

Rnd 1: *K2, p2tog; rep from * around. (33 sts)

Rnd 2: *K2, p1; rep from * around.

Rnd 3: *K2tog, p1; rep from * around. (22 sts)

Rnd 4: Inc 1 st in each st. (44 sts)

Rnds 5–6: Knit.

Rnd 7: [K10, inc 1 st in next st] 4 times. (48 sts)

Work even in St st until pants measures 2¾ inches from beg.

Cut yarn.

Right Leg

Fold pants so high part of bib is at center front. Locate center front st. Place 24 sts to left of center on holder, divide rem 24 sts equally onto 3 dpn.

Join yarn at inseam.

Work even in St st for 30 rnds.

Inc Rnd 1: [Inc in first st, k11] twice. (26 sts)

Knit 6 rnds.

Inc Rnd 2: [Inc in first st, k12] twice. (28 sts)

Knit 6 rnds.

Inc Rnd 3: [Inc in first st, k13] twice. (30 sts)

Knit 4 rnds, purl 2 rnds.

Bind off purlwise.

Left Leg

Sl sts from holder onto 3 dpn. Work as for first leg.

Bag

Cast on 44 sts and divide onto 3 dpn, having 15 sts on each of first 2 needles and 14 sts on 3rd needle. Join without twisting, pm between first and last st.

Rnd 1: Purl.

Rnd 2: K7, bind off 8 sts for first handle, k13, bind off 8 sts for 2nd handle, k6. (28 sts)

Rnd 3: K7, cast on 2 sts, k14, cast on 2 sts, k7. (32 sts)

Rnds 4–20: Knit.

Rnd 21: P2tog, p12, [p2tog] twice, p12, p2tog. (28 sts)

Bind off knitwise.

Fold bag in half.

Sew bound-off edges tog for base of bag. ●

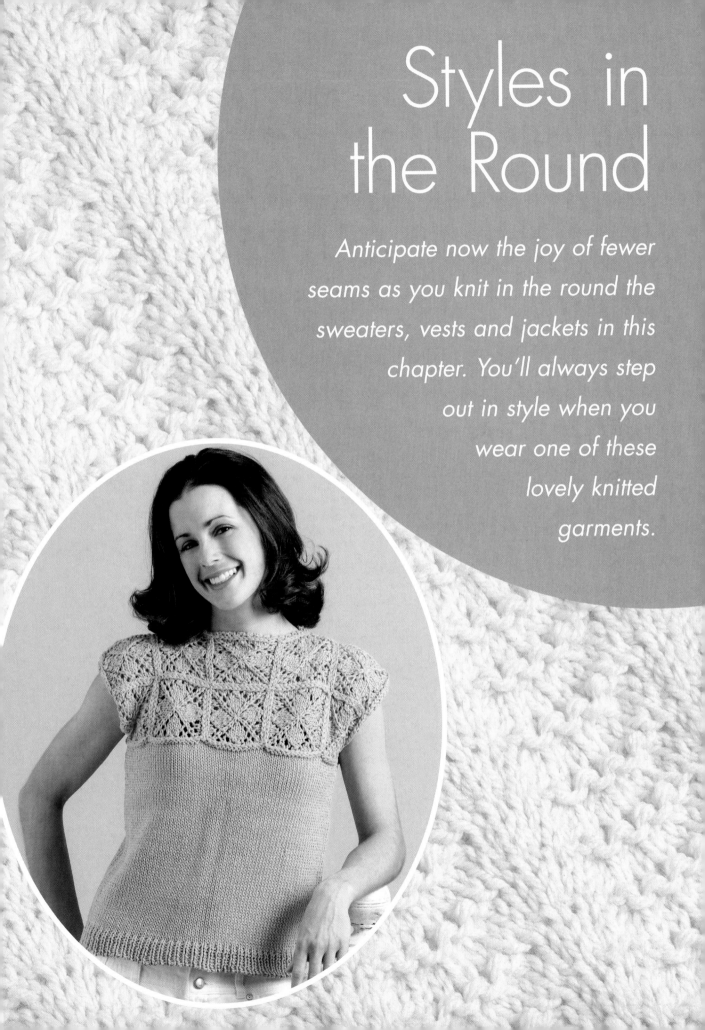

Styles in the Round

Anticipate now the joy of fewer seams as you knit in the round the sweaters, vests and jackets in this chapter. You'll always step out in style when you wear one of these lovely knitted garments.

Counterpane Yoke Sweater

Design by Uyvonne Bigham

Squares in an antique counterpane were the inspiration for this summery top.

Skill Level

INTERMEDIATE

Size

Woman's small (medium, large) Instructions are given for smallest size, with larger sizes in parentheses. When only 1 number is given, it applies to all sizes.

Finished Measurements

Chest: 35½ (37½, 40) inches

Length: 20 inches

Materials

4 MEDIUM Plymouth Fantasy Naturale 100 percent mercerized cotton worsted weight yarn (140 yds/100g per skein): 6 (6, 7) skeins light coral #4548

- Size 6 (4mm) or 7 (4.5mm) 29-inch circular needles for ribbing
- Size 7 (4.5mm), 8 (5mm) or 9 (5.5mm) set of 5 double-pointed and 29-inch circular needles or size needed to obtain gauge for body and yoke motifs

Gauge

For size small only: 18 sts and 25 rows = 4 inches/10cm in St st with size 7 needles

For size medium only: 17 sts and 24 rows = 4 inches/10cm in St st with size 8 needles

For size large only: 16 sts and 22 rows = 4 inches/10cm in St st with size 9 needles

To save time, take time to check gauge.

Pattern Notes

All sizes are worked in the same way; differences in size come from needle size and gauge difference.

Motifs for yoke are worked separately, then sewn together to form yoke.

It may be necessary to use a larger needle when binding off motifs.

Counterpane Motif
Make 20

With size 7 (8, 9) dpn, make a sl knot.

Working in center of knot, [draw up a st, yo] 4 times. (8 sts)

Divide sts onto 4 needles. Join without twisting, pm between first and last st.

Rnd 1 and all uneven-numbered rnds: Knit.

Rnd 2: *K1, yo; rep from * around. (16 sts)

Rnd 4: *K1, yo, k3, yo; rep from * around. (24 sts)

Rnd 6: *K1, yo, k5, yo; rep from * around. (32 sts)

Rnd 8: *[K1, yo] twice, k2tog, k1, ssk, yo, k1, yo; rep from * around. (40 sts)

Rnd 10: *K1, yo, k3, yo, k3tog, k3, yo, k3, yo; rep from * around. (48 sts)

Bind off loosely.

If necessary, tighten or sew center of motif closed.

Yoke

Sew 5 motifs tog to form a long strip, allowing bound-off edges of motif to fall to RS of work.

Continued on page 92

[Knit 5 rnds, rep dec rnd] 3 times. (132, 144, 156, 168 sts) [Knit 7 rnds, rep dec rnd] twice. (108,120,132,144 sts) Removing extra markers, pm at beg of rnd and after 54th (60th, 66th, 72nd) st to mark side seams.

Begin body shaping

Knit 3 (3, 1, 1) rnds.

Next rnd: Inc by working M1 before and after each marker. (4 sts inc)

[Rep inc rnd every 4th (4th, 4th, 2nd) rnd] 7 (9, 10, 3) times, then [every 6th (0, 0, 4th) rnd] 1 (0, 0, 4) times. (144, 160, 176, 192 sts)

Work even until body measures 15 (15½, 16, 16) inches.

Divide for front and back

Work in rows from this point.

Next row: K 72 (80, 88, 96) sts, place rem sts on hold for front.

Back

Shape armhole

Bind off 6 (7, 7, 7) sts at beg of next 2 rows. (60, 66, 78, 82 sts)

Dec row (RS): K1, skp, k to last 3 sts, k2tog, k1.

Next row: Purl.

[Rep last 2 rows] 1 (3, 5, 7) times. (56, 58, 62, 66 sts)

Work even until armhole measures 8 (8, 8, 9) inches.

Place sts on 3 holders, having 15 (15, 16, 17) sts for each shoulder and 26 (28, 30, 32) sts for back neck.

Front

Work as for back until armhole measures 4 (4, 4, 5) inches, ending with a WS row.

Begin neck shaping

K 22 (23, 25, 27) sts, join 2nd

ball of yarn and bind off next 12 sts, k to end of row.

Working both sides of neck with separate balls of yarn, bind off at each neck edge [2 sts] 2 (3, 4, 5) times.

[Dec 1 st each side of neck every other row] 3 (2, 1, 0) times.

Work even on rem 15 (15, 16, 17) sts until armhole measures same as for back.

Join front and back shoulders with 3-needle bind-off.

Sleeves

Beg at cuff with dpn and 1 strand of each yarn held tog, cast on 48 (48, 54, 54) sts. Join without twisting, pm between first and last st.

Next rnd: Working in Seed St, pm after every 8th (8th, 9th, 9th) st.

Work 1 more rnd Seed St, then knit 7 rnds.

Dec rnd: [K to 1 st before marker, CDD, reposition marker] 6 times.

Knit 7 rnds, rep dec rnd. (24, 24, 30, 30 sts)

Remove all markers except one designating end of rnd.

Knit 5 (3, 5, 3) rnds.

Working in St st, [inc 1 st each side of marker every 6th (6th, 6th, 4th) rnd] 10 (15, 6, 2) times, then [every 8th (0, 8th, 6th] rnd] 3 (0, 7, 14) times.

Working in St st, k 5 (3, 5, 3) rnds even. (50, 54, 56, 62 sts)

Work even until sleeve measures 19 (19¾, 20¼, 20¼) inches.

Shape sleeve cap

Work in rows from this point.

Bind off 6 (7, 7, 7) sts at beg of next 2 rows.

[Dec 1 st each end every other row] 2 (4, 6, 8) times, then [every 4th row] 7 (5, 4, 6) times, and finally [every 6th row] 0 (1, 1, 0) times. (20 sts)

Purl 1 row.

Bind off 2 sts at beg of next 4 rows.

Bind off rem 12 sts.

Neck Edging

With shorter circular needle, pick up and k 2 sts for every 3 rows and 1 st for every st around neck edge. Join, pm between first and last st.

Knit 5 rnds.

Bind off loosely.

Sew sleeves into armholes. ●

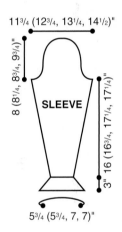

11¾ (12¾, 13¼, 14½)"

8 (8¼, 8¾, 9¾)"

SLEEVE

3" 16 (16¾, 17¼, 17¼)"

5¾ (5¾, 7, 7)"

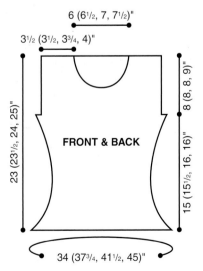

6 (6½, 7, 7½)"

3½ (3½, 3¾, 4)"

23 (23½, 24, 25)"

8 (8, 8, 9)"

FRONT & BACK

15 (15½, 16, 16)"

34 (37¾, 41½, 45)"

Zip Vest

Design by Diane Zangl

For elegant or casual wear, this zippered vest is a perfect match for cargo pants or to add pizzazz to a simple dress.

Skill Level

■■■□
INTERMEDIATE

Size

Woman's small (medium, large, extra-large) Instructions are given for smallest size, with larger sizes in parentheses. When only 1 number is given, it applies to all sizes.

Finished Measurements

Chest: 36 (40, 44, 48) inches

Armhole depth:
8½ (9, 9½, 10) inches

Side to underarm:
11 (11½, 11½, 12) inches

Materials

5
BULKY Plymouth Alpaca Bouclé 90 percent alpaca/10 percent nylon bulky weight yarn (70 yds/50g per ball): 7 (8, 10, 12) balls burnt orange #17 (MC)

4
MEDIUM Plymouth Indiecita Alpaca 100 percent Peruvian Alpaca worsted weight yarn (100 yds/50g per ball): 2 balls black #500 (CC)

- Size 4 (3.5mm) 29-inch circular needle
- Size 5 (3.75mm) 29-inch circular needle
- Size 6 (4mm) 29-inch circular needle or size needed to obtain gauge
- Stitch holders
- Stitch markers
- 16- (18-, 18-, 18-) inch separating zipper
- Matching sewing thread

Gauge

13 sts and 21 rows = 4 inches/10cm in rev St st with MC and larger needles

To save time, take time to check gauge.

Special Abbreviation

M1 (Make 1): Make a backward lp and place on RH needle.

Pattern Notes

Rev St st is used for the body and collar of the vest. Front edges and collar are edged with I-cord. A casing and drawstring finish the lower edge.

As it is difficult to see the sts with this yarn, mark the purl side of the body and collar as the RS of your work. You may want to carry a waste strand of CC along the edges of body, armhole and collar. This will make it easier when picking up sts for the edgings.

Body

With CC and size 5 needles, cast on 154 (174, 190, 208) sts. Work even in St st for 1¾ inch, ending with a WS row.

Form casing

With size 4 needles, pick up each cast-on st at lower edge. Fold casing in half, bringing needle with picked-up sts to back of work. Knit sts will be on outside.

With opposite end of size 5 needle, k2tog (1 st from each needle) across row.

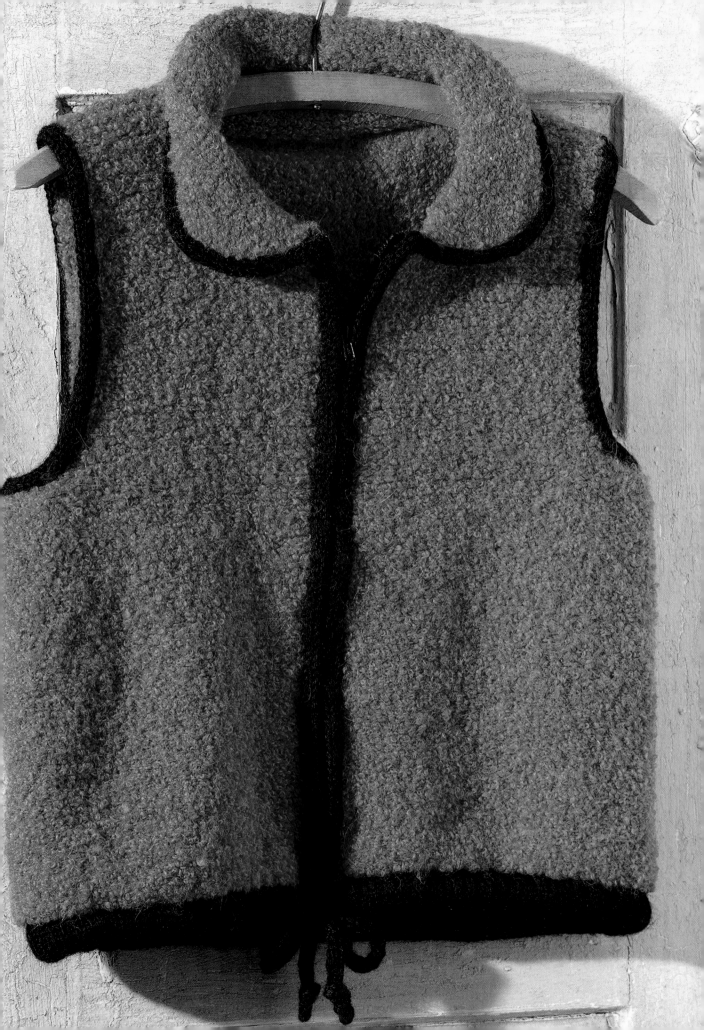

Change to size 6 needles and MC.

Next row (WS): P, dec 38 (42, 46, 52) sts evenly. (116, 132, 144, 156 sts)

Work even in rev St st until body measures 11 (11½, 11½, 12) inches, ending with a WS row.

Divide for fronts and back

P 24 (26, 29, 30) sts and place on holder, bind off next 10 (14, 14, 18) sts for right underarm, p 48 (52, 58, 60) sts for back, bind off next 10 (14, 14, 18) sts for left underarm, p to end of row and sl front sts to holder. Mark last row of fronts and back. Keep track of rows from this point, as it is almost impossible to count them in your work.

Back

With WS facing, join yarn at left underarm. Working on back sts only, [dec 1 st at each end every other row] 3 (3, 4, 4) times. (42, 46, 50, 52 sts)

Work even in rev St st until armhole measures 8½ (9, 9½, 10) inches, ending with a WS row.

Shape shoulders

Short rows: P to last 3 (4, 4, 4) sts, turn, sl 1, k to last 3 (4, 4, 4) sts, turn.

Sl 1, p to last 6 (8, 8, 8) sts, turn, sl 1, k to last 6 (8, 8, 8) sts turn.

Sl 1, p to last 10 (11, 12, 13) sts, turn, sl 1, k to last 10 (11, 12, 13) sts turn.

Place 10 (11, 12, 13) sts at each side on separate holders for shoulders.

Place rem 22 (24, 26, 26) sts on another holder for back neck.

Fronts

Sl sts of fronts to larger needle. With WS facing, join a separate ball of yarn to each front. Working on both fronts with separate balls of yarn, [dec 1 st at each arm edge every other row] 3 (3, 4, 4) times. (21, 23, 25, 26 sts)

Work even until armholes measure 6 (6½, 6½, 6½) inches, ending with a WS row.

Shape neckline

Next row (RS): Place 8 (9, 10, 10) sts at each neck edge on holders.

[Dec 1 st at each side of neck every row] 3 times. (10, 11, 12, 13 sts)

Work even until armhole measures same as for back.

Shape shoulders as for back, using short rows.

Join shoulders, using 3-needle bind-off method.

Collar

With RS facing using MC and size 6 needles, k across 8 (9, 10, 10) sts of right front neck, pick up and k 12 (12, 16, 18) sts along right neck edge, pm, k 22 (24, 26, 26) sts of back neck, pm, pick up and k 12 (12, 16, 18) sts along left neck edge, k 8 (9, 10, 10) sts of left front neck. (62, 66, 78, 82 sts)

Shape back of collar

P to right shoulder marker, turn, sl 1, k to left shoulder marker, turn.

Sl 1, p to 3 sts beyond marker, turn, sl 1, k to 3 sts beyond marker, turn.

Sl 1, p to 6 sts beyond marker, turn, sl 1, k to 6 sts beyond marker, turn.

Sl 1, p to end of row. Remove markers.

Work even in rev St st until collar measures 2 inches at front edge.

[Dec 1 st each end every other row] 3 times. (56, 60, 72, 76 sts)

Place sts on holder.

Finishing
Front I-cord edging

With RS facing, beg at lower right front corner above casing using CC and size 5 needles, pick up and k 1 st in each row along front edge, pm and record number of sts, pick up and p 1 st in each row along short edge of collar, pm and record sts, [p3, M1] along long edge of collar, pick up and p along short edge of collar same number of sts as on opposite edge, pick up and k along left front edge same number of sts as for right front. Cut yarn.

Return to right front corner and cast on 4 sts to LH needle. *K3, ssk, sl sts back to LH needle. Rep from * until all picked-up sts have been worked.

Armhole edging

Beg at center of underarm with CC and size 5 needles, pick up and k 1 st in each bound-off st of underarm and 1 st in each row of armhole. Do not cut yarn.

Cast on 4 sts to RH needle, sl these sts to LH needle.

Rep from * as for front edging until all picked-up sts have been worked. Cut yarn and sew last row of sts to cast-on sts.

Drawstring

Cast on 4 sts. *K4, replace sts to LH needle. Rep from * until cord measures approx 48 (52, 56, 60) inches long. Bind off.

Thread drawstring through casing. Tie an overhand knot in each end.

Sew in zipper. ●

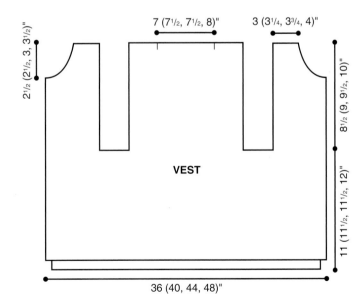

KNITTING IN THE ROUND

3rd, 3rd) rnd] 10 (1, 4, 1) times, then every 0 (2nd, 2nd, 2nd) rnd 0 (11, 8, 12) times.

At the same time, when yoke measures 5½ (6, 6½, 7) inches above center front marker, begin front neck shaping.

Neck shaping

Work to center 6 (6, 8, 8) sts, place center 6 (6, 8, 8) sts on hold, turn.

Working in rows from this point, [dec 1 st at each side of neck every other row] 3 times.

Work until raglan decs are complete. (32, 32, 36, 40 sts)

Piece should measure approx 23 (24, 25, 26) inches. Leave rem sts on needle and cut yarn.

Collar

With 16-inch circular needle and RS facing, pick up and k 5 (6, 6, 6) sts along left neck edge, knit 6 (6, 8, 8) sts from front neck holder, pick up and k 5 (6, 6, 6) sts along right neck edge, k rem sts from needle. (48, 50, 56, 60 sts)

Join, pm between first and last st.

Work even in St st for 2 (2, 3, 3) inches, then work 4 rnds in k1, p1 rib.

Bind off in ribbing.

Finishing

Sew underarm sleeve sts to underarm body sts, using Kitchener method. ●

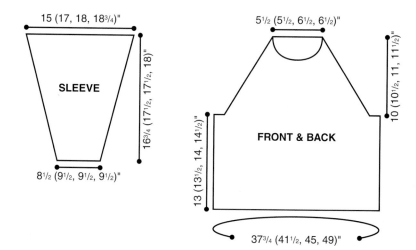

15 (17, 18, 18¾)"

SLEEVE

16¾ (17½, 17½, 18)"

8½ (9½, 9½, 9½)"

5½ (5½, 6½, 6½)"

10 (10½, 11, 11½)"

FRONT & BACK

13 (13½, 14, 14½)"

37¾ (41½, 45, 49)"

Grapevine Pullover

Design by Sara Louise Harper

A simple lace pattern creates the look of cables in this comfortable pullover.

Skill Level

INTERMEDIATE

Size

Woman's small (medium, large, extra-large) Instructions are given for smallest size, with larger sizes in parentheses. When only 1 number is given, it applies to all sizes.

Finished Measurements

Chest: 40 (44, 48, 52) inches

Armhole depth: 9 (10, 10, 11) inches

Side to underarm: 16 (16, 17, 17) inches

Sleeve length: 19 (20, 21, 21½) inches

Materials

4 MEDIUM Plymouth Galway Highland Heather 100 percent wool worsted weight yarn (210 yds/100g per skein): 8 (9, 10, 11) skeins light green heather #738

- Size 8 (5mm) 32-inch circular needle or size needed to obtain gauge
- Stitch markers
- Stitch holders
- Tapestry needle

Gauge

18 sts and 27 rows = 4 inches/10cm in Grapevine pat

To save time, take time to check gauge.

Pattern Stitch

Grapevine (multiple of 8 sts + 6)

Rnd 1 and all odd-numbered rnds: Knit.

Rnd 2: *K2, k2tog, k1, yo, k1, ssk; rep from * across, end last rep k6.

Rnd 4: K1, k2tog, *k1, [yo, k1] twice, ssk, k2tog; rep from * across, end last rep k1, yo, k2.

Rnd 6: K3, yo, k3, *yo, k1, ssk, k1, yo, k3; rep from * across.

Rnd 8: K5, k2tog, k1, yo, k1, ssk, *k2, k2tog, k1, yo, k1, ssk; rep from * across, end last rep k4.

Rnd 10: K4, *k2tog, k1, [yo, k1] twice, ssk; rep from * across, end last rep k3.

Rnd 12: K3, k2tog, *k1, yo, k3, yo, k1, k2tog; rep from * across, end last rep k2.

Rep Rnds/Rows 1–12 for pat.

Pattern Notes

Garment is worked in rnds to the underarm, divided for front and back, then worked back and forth to shoulders.

Sleeves are worked back and forth.

When working in rows, purl all WS rows.

The rows/rnds of Grapevine pat do not contain the same number of stitches. To check that pattern is maintained, be sure that end sts are correct on every row/rnd.

Because pat st count varies, count is given only at strategic points.

Body

Cast on 188 (204, 220, 236) sts. Join without twisting, pm between first and last st.

Work even in k2, p2 rib for 1 inch, ending with a WS row.

Next rnd: Work Rnd 1 of Grapevine pat across 94 (102, 110, 188) sts, pm, rep Rnd 1 on rem 94 (102, 110, 188) sts.

Work even until body measures 16 (16, 17, 17) inches, ending with an odd-numbered rnd.

Divide for front and back

Work to marker, place rem sts on holder for front.

Work in rows from this point.

Work even until armhole measures 9 (10, 10, 11) inches, ending with a RS row.

Bind off all sts.

Front

Sl sts from holder to needle.

Beg with a RS row, work even until armhole measures approx 6 (7, 7, 8) inches, ending with Row 4 of pat. (83, 90, 97, 104 sts)

Shape neckline

Next row: Work across 32 (35, 38, 41) sts, join 2nd ball of yarn and bind off center 19 (20, 21, 22) sts, work to end of row.

[Bind off 2 sts at each side of neck every other row] 3 times.

Work even until armhole measures same as for back.

Bind off all sts on a WS row.

Sleeves

Cast on 30 (34, 34, 38) sts.

Work even in k2, p2 rib for 1 inch, ending with a WS row.

Set up pat: K0 (2, 2, 0), pm, work Row 1 of Grapevine pat, pm, k0 (2, 2, 0).

[Inc 1 st each end every other row] 2 (3, 2, 1) times.

Work new sts in St st until there are enough to work into Grapevine pat.

[Inc 1 st each end of needle every 4th row] 13 (13, 12, 15) times, then every 5th (6th, 6th, 6th) row 10 (10, 12, 14) times.

Work even until sleeve measures 19 (20, 21, 21½) inches.

Bind off all sts on WS.

Seam shoulders seams.

Neck Band

With RS facing, pick up and k 88 (92, 96, 100) sts evenly around neckline.

Work even in k2, p2 rib until neck band measures 1½ inches.

Bind off loosely in pat.

Finishing

Sew sleeves into armholes.

Sew sleeve seam. ●

6¾ (7½, 8¼, 9)"

6½ (7, 7½, 8)"

9 (10, 10, 11)"

25 (26, 27, 28)"

FRONT & BACK

15 (15, 16, 16)"

1"

40 (44, 48, 52)"

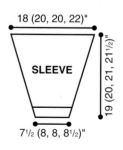

18 (20, 20, 22)"

SLEEVE

19 (20, 21, 21½)"

7½ (8, 8, 8½)"

times, then [every other row] 4 times. (186, 198, 210, 222 sts)

Joining row: Pm, cast on 5 steek sts, pm, work to end of rnd.

Work even in Diagonal pat until body measures 14 (14½, 15, 15) inches.

Beg armhole steeks

Next rnd: Keeping to established pat, work across 39 (41, 44, 47) sts, bind off 16 sts for underarm, work across 78 (84, 90, 96) sts, bind off 16 sts for underarm, work across 39 (41, 44, 47) sts. (156, 166, 178, 190 sts)

Next rnd: Cast on 5 sts above each bound-off armhole area for armhole steeks.

[Dec 1 st each side of each armhole every round] 4 (5, 5, 6) times. (140, 146, 158, 166 sts)

Work even until armhole measures 6½ (6½, 6¾, 7) inches, ending 8 (8, 8, 9) sts before end of last rnd.

Bind off next 21 (21, 21, 23) sts. This includes steek sts plus 8 (8, 8, 9) sts at each neck edge.

Work in rows from this point.

Bind off 3 sts at each neck edge, then 2 (1, 2, 1) sts at each neck edge.

[Dec 1 st each at each neck edge every other row] 3 (3, 2, 3) times. (19, 21, 24, 24 sts left on each side of neck.)

Work even until armhole measures 9½ (9½, 9¾, 10) inches.

Bind off all sts.

Sleeves

With MC and smaller dpn, cast on 56 (60, 62, 62) sts.

Join without twisting, pm between first and last st.

Working in Diagonal pat, [inc 1 st each side of marker every 4th rnd] 17 (18 17, 19) times, working added sts into pat and changing to longer needles when necessary. (90, 96, 96, 102 sts)

Work even until sleeve measures 16 (16½, 16½, 17) inches.

Shape sleeve cap

Work even in rows from this point for 1½ inches.

[Dec 1 st each end every other row] 4 (5, 5, 5) times. (82, 86, 86, 92 sts)

Bind off in pat.

Sew and cut steeks.

Sew shoulder seams.

Sleeve Bands

With CC and larger dpn, pick up and k 1 st in each cast-on sleeve st.

Purl 9 rnds.

Bind off; band will roll naturally to the inside.

Front Bands

With CC and larger circular needles, pick up and k 3 sts for each 1 inch around entire front opening, adding 2nd needle when necessary.

Purl 9 rnds.

Bind off; band will roll naturally to the inside.

Finishing

Sew sleeves into armholes.

Turn steeks to inside and stitch in place.

Sew hook-and-eye closures to inside of front bands. ●

STITCH KEY
☐ K on RS, p on WS
⊟ P on RS, k on WS

DIAGONAL ILLUSION CHART

Row 23: K5, *k10, yo, CDD, yo, k3; rep from * across, end last rep k12.

Row 24: Rep Row 12.

Rep Rows 1–24 for pat.

Pattern Note

Circular needles are used to accommodate large number of sts. Do not join; work in rows.

Body

Cast on 161 (177, 193, 209) sts. Knit 8 rows.

Work even in Diamonds pat until body measures 15 (16, 16, 16) inches, ending with a WS row.

Divide for fronts and back

Next row: Work across 39 (43, 47, 51) sts and place on holder for right front, work across 83 (91, 99, 107) sts, place rem 39 (43, 47, 51) sts on 2nd holder for left front.

Back

Work even in established pat until armhole measures 8½ (9½, 10½, 11½) inches, ending with a WS row.

Next row: Work across 31 (34, 37 40) sts, join 2nd ball of yarn and bind off next 21 (23, 25, 27) sts, work to end of row.

Working on both sides of neck with separate balls of yarn, work even until armhole measures 9 (9, 10, 11) inches.

Bind off all sts.

Right Front

Sl sts from holder to needle. With WS facing, join yarn at arm edge.

Work even in established pat until armhole measures 6 (6, 7,

k1, k2tog, yo, k10; rep from * across, end last rep k1, yo, ssk, k1, k2tog, yo, k6.

Row 10: Rep Row 2.

Row 11: K5, *k2, yo, CDD, yo, k11; rep from * across, end last rep k2, yo, CDD, yo, k7.

Row 12: K7, p3, k2, *k3, p3, k5, p3, k2; rep from * across, end last rep k5.

Row 13: K5, *k9, k2tog, yo, k1, yo, ssk, k2; rep from * across, end last rep k12.

Row 14: K8, p1, k3, *k2, p5, k5, p1, k3; rep from * across, end last rep k5.

Row 15: K5, *k8, k2tog, yo, k3, yo, ssk, k1; rep from * across, end last rep k12.

Row 16: K8, p1, k3, *k1, p7, k4, p1, k3; rep from * across, end last rep k5.

Row 17: K5, *k7, k2tog, yo, k5, yo, ssk; rep from * across, end last rep k12.

Row 18: K8, p1, k3, *p9, k3, p1, k3; rep from * across, end last rep k5.

Row 19: K5, *k8, yo, ssk, k3, k2tog, yo, k1; rep from * across, end last rep k12.

Row 20: Rep Row 16.

Row 21: K5, *k9, yo, ssk, k1, k2tog, yo, k2; rep from * across, end last rep k12.

Row 22: Rep Row 14.

8) inches, ending with a WS row.

Shape neckline

Next row: Bind off 4 (3, 4, 3) sts, work to end of row.

[Bind off 2 sts at neck edge every other row] 3 (4, 4, 5) times. (21, 23, 25, 27 sts)

Work even until armhole measures same as for back.

Bind off all sts.

Left Front

Work as for right front, reversing shaping.

Sleeves

Cast on 33 (33, 37, 37) sts. Knit 8 rows.

Set up pat: K3 (3, 5, 5), pm, work Diamonds pat across next 27 sts, pm, k3 (3, 5, 5).

Keeping sts between markers in Diamonds pat, and rem sts in garter st, [inc 1 st each end every other row] (2, 2, 3) times, then [every 3rd row] 12 (14, 15, 16) times, and finally [every 10th row] 6 times. (73, 77, 83, 87 sts)

Work added sts into Diamonds pat only when there are enough sts for a complete rep.

Work even until sleeve measures 18 (19, 20, 21) inches.

Bind off in pat.

Sew shoulder seams.

Neck Band

With RS facing beg at front edge, pick up and k 68 (72, 76, 80) sts evenly around neckline.

Knit 5 rows.

Bind off loosely.

Button Band

With RS facing, pick up and k 70 (74, 79, 82) sts along left front edge.

Knit 6 rows.

Bind off loosely.

Buttonhole Band

Pick up and k as for button band, knit 3 rows. Mark band for 6 (6, 7, 7) buttonholes, evenly spaced.

Buttonhole row: [K to marker, yo, k2tog] 6 (6, 7, 7) times, k to end of row.

Knit 2 rows.

Bind off loosely.

Finishing

Sew sleeves into armholes.

Sew on buttons. ●

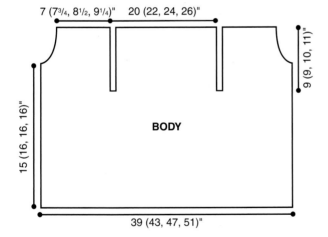

BODY

7 (7¾, 8½, 9¼)" 20 (22, 24, 26)"

9 (9, 10, 11)"

15 (16, 16, 16)"

39 (43, 47, 51)"

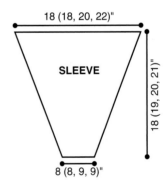

SLEEVE

18 (18, 20, 22)"

18 (19, 20, 21)"

8 (8, 9, 9)"

Row 2: K2, *p2, k2, rep from * across.

Rep Rows 1 and 2 until ribbing measures approx 1½ inches, ending with Row 1.

Beg on RS with a p row and keeping 1 selvage st at each edge in St st, work in rev St st until body measures 8 inches, ending with a p row.

Shape sides

With k side facing, pm after st #29 (32, 35, 38) and st #88 (97, 106, 115).

Dec row (WS): *K to 2 sts before marker, k2tog, k1, ssk, rep from * once more, work to end. (4 sts dec)

[Work as established until body measures 3 inches above dec row, ending with a p row. Rep dec row] twice. (106, 118, 130, 142 sts)

Work even until body measures 14 inches from beg, ending with a p row.

Divide for front and back

Work across first 23 (25, 26, 29) sts and place on holder for left front, bind off 7 (9, 13, 13) sts for underarm, work to 3 (4, 6, 6) sts before 2nd marker. Turn and place rem sts on 2nd holder for right front.

Back

Working on back sts only, [dec 1 st at each armhole edge every k row] 5 times.

Work even on rem 36 (40, 42, 48) sts until armhole measures 8½ (9, 9½, 10) inches.

Shape shoulders

Rows 1 and 2: Work to 3 sts from end, W/T.

Rows 3 and 4: Work to

2 (3, 3, 4) sts from previous wrap, W/T.

Rows 5 and 6: Work to 2 (3, 2, 4) sts from previous wrap, W/T.

Rows 7 and 8: Work across row, working each wrap tog with its matching st.

Place all sts on holder, marking center 22 (22, 26, 26) sts for back neck.

Right Front

With WS facing, join yarn at underarm and bind off next 7 (9, 13, 13) sts, work to end of row.

Keeping 1 st at each edge in St st, [dec 1 st at armhole edge every k row] 5 times.

Work even on rem 18 (20, 21, 24) sts until armhole measures 5½ (6, 6, 6½) inches, ending with a k row.

Shape neck

Next row: Bind off 8 (8, 10, 10) sts purlwise, work to end of row.

[Dec 1 st at neck edge every k row] 3 times.

Work even on rem 7 (9, 8, 11) sts until armhole measures same as for back.

Shape shoulder as for back.

Join shoulders

Bind off front and back shoulder sts tog as follows: Sl back shoulder sts to a spare needle. Hold needles containing shoulder sts parallel, with RS tog. With 3rd needle, k first st on front and back needles tog, *k next st on both needles tog, bind off 1, rep from * until all sts are worked.

Fasten off.

Left Front

With p side facing, attach yarn

at underarm, p to front edge.

Work as for right front, reversing shaping.

Sleeves

With Size 9 dpn, cast on 24 (24, 28, 28) sts. Join without twisting, pm between first and last st.

Work even in k2, p2 rib until cuff measures 3 inches, changing to size 10 needles and inc 4 (4, 6, 8) sts evenly on last rnd. (28, 28, 34, 36 sts)

Note: *Sleeves may be worked in rev St st throughout, or in St st and turned at end, as preferred.*

Work 1 rnd even.

[Inc 1 st each side of marker every 4th rnd] 6 (7, 6, 6) times, then [every 6th rnd] 6 times. (52, 54, 58, 60 sts)

Work even until sleeve measures 20¾ (20¼, 19¾, 19) inches or desired length, ending 3 (4, 6, 6) sts before marker on last rnd.

Shape cap

Bind off next 7 (9, 13, 13) sts, work in rows from this point.

[Dec 1 st each end every k row] 4 times.

Bind off all sts purlwise on next row.

Right Front Band

Beg at lower edge with size 9 needle and p side (RS) facing, pick up and k 2 sts for every 3 rows to neck edge.

Sl first st of every row, work 5 rows of garter st.

Bind off all sts purlwise on next row.

Left Front Band

Beg at neck edge work as for right front, making sure to pick up same number of sts.

Collar

With size 8 needle, beg at right front with p side (RS) facing, pick up and k 4 sts across top of front band, 8 (8, 10, 10) sts across front neck, 11 sts along side of neck, pm, k 22 (22, 26, 26) back neck sts inc 2 sts evenly, pm, pick up and k around left side of neck to match right side. (70, 70, 78, 78 sts)

Size L (XL) only: On Row 1, move each marker 2 sts toward back. (24 back neck sts between markers)

Row 1: *K2, p2, rep from * to last 6 sts, k2tog, [yo] twice, p2tog, k2. (buttonhole)

Beg shaping

P2, k1, [k1, p1] in yo, p1, *k2, p2, rep from * to 2nd marker, wrap first st after marker and turn. Work back to other marker, W/T.

**Maintaining established rib throughout, work to previous wrapped st, work wrap and st tog, rib 3 more sts, W/T. Rep from ** until 2 sts rem unworked at each end, work to end of row. Change to size 10 needle, work across all sts.

Next row: Work to 2nd marker, W/T. Work back to other marker, W/T.

Rep from ** until 2 sts rem unworked at each end, work to end of row. Turn and bind off all sts in pat, working last wrap and st tog as you go.

Finishing

Sew in sleeves.

Sew button on left front to match buttonhole.

Block lightly. ●

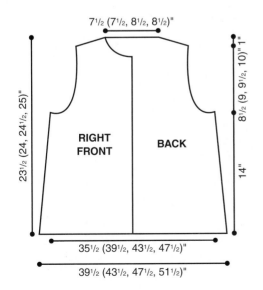

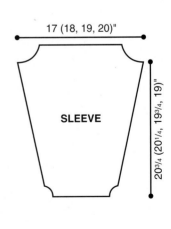

Year-Round Accessories

For a weekend of fun knitting, make one of these quick-to-stitch accessories for yourself or your children. They'll love the colorful hats, scarves, and other accessories, and you'll enjoy every stitch as you knit in the round.

sts. Join without twisting, pm between first and last st. Marker will be center back of hat.

Next rnd: [K2, p2] 12 times, with RS facing, place one earflap behind work. Working in k2, p2 rib, work 1 st from main needle and 1 earflap st tog until all earflap sts have been joined. Work in rib over next 60 sts, join 2nd earflap as for first, work in rib to end of rnd.

Work even in Mock Cable pat for 1½ inches.

Next rnd: Knit, inc 2 sts evenly. (150 sts)

Work even in St st until hat measures 5½ inches above cast-on edge.

Dec rnd: *K13, k2tog; rep from * around.

Knit 1 rnd.

Next rnd: *K12, k2tog; rep from * around.

Knit 1 rnd.

Continue to dec in this manner, having 1 less st between decs until 10 sts rem.

Cut yarn, leaving a 10-inch end.

Draw end through rem sts twice and pull tightly.

Braids

Cut 18 strands of yarn, each 24 inches long; separate into 3 sets of 6 strands each.

With crochet hook, pull 1 set through top of hat and adjust ends. Divide group into 3 strands of 4 each and braid tightly to approx 3 inches.

Tie an overhand knot in end.

Trim tassel to desired length.

Rep at bottom of each earflap with rem 2 sets of strands.

Glittens

With larger dpn, cast on 52 st. Divide evenly onto 4 needles. Join without twisting, pm between first and last st.

Work even in Mock Cable pat for 2¾ inches.

Next rnd: Knit, inc 4 sts evenly. (56 sts)

Work even in St st until glitten measures 5½ inches, or desired length to thumb.

Beg thumb

Right glitten only: With a 12-inch strand of waste yarn, k first 6 sts, drop waste yarn. Sl these 6 sts back to LH needle and k them again with working yarn, k to end of rnd.

Left glitten only: K to last 6 sts, k6 with waste yarn, drop waste yarn. Sl these 6 sts back to LH needle and k them again with working yarn.

Both glittens: Work even for 1½ inches.

Beg finger (both glittens worked alike)

Next rnd: K6 and place on holder, k to last 6 sts and place on 2nd holder. On following rnd, cast on 4 sts to last needle over held sts. (48 sts)

Knit 2 rnds.

Next rnd: Rearrange sts by slipping 2 sts of last needle to first needle. Mark new beg of rnd.

Work even until glitten measures 1¾ inch above 4 cast-on sts.

Dec rnd: *K6, k2tog; rep from * around. (42 sts)

Knit 4 rnds.

Dec rnd: *K5, k2tog; rep from * around. (36 sts)

Knit 4 rnds.

Dec rnd: *K4, k2tog; rep from * around. (30 sts)

Knit 4 rnds.

Dec rnd: *Sl 1, k2tog, psso; rep from * around. (10 sts)

Cut yarn, leaving a 10-inch end.

Draw end through rem sts twice and pull tightly.

Thumb

With smaller dpn and without removing waste yarn, pick up 6 sts on lower edge of thumb and 7 lps on upper edge. Remove contrast yarn.

With larger dpn, k across 6 lower sts.

With 2nd needle, pick up and k 2 sts along side of opening, then k across 4 upper loops.

With 3rd needle, k across rem 3 loops, pick up and k 3 more sts along rem side of opening. (18 sts)

Work even in St st until thumb measures 2½ inches or desired length.

Dec rnd: *Sl 1, k2tog, psso; rep from * around. (9 sts)

Cut yarn, leaving a 10-inch end.

Draw end through rem sts twice and pull tightly.

Index Finger

Place st from first holder on 1 larger dpn. Attach yarn and k these 6 sts onto first needle.

With 2nd needle, pick up and k 1 st at side of opening, 4 sts along cast-on edge and 1 st at rem side of opening.

Place sts from 2nd holder on 3rd needle and k them. (18 sts)

Mark first st on first needle as beg of rnd.

Work even in St st until finger measures 3 inches or desired length.

Dec rnd: *Sl 1, k2tog, psso; rep from * around. (9 sts)

Cut yarn, leaving a 10-inch end.

Draw end through rem sts twice and pull tightly. ●

Rnd 19: *K1, sl 1, ssk, psso; rep from * around. (14 sts)

Rnds 20 and 21: Knit

Rnd 22: *Sl 1, ssk, psso; rep from * to last 2 sts, ssk. (4 sts)

Cut yarn, leaving a 12-inch end. Draw end through rem sts twice and pull tightly.

Scarf

Right Front

With larger needle, cast on 32 sts. Beg with a p row, work in St st for 7 rows.

Mark beg of next row and k to end.

Work even in St st for 110 rows more. Mark last row.

Beg neck shaping

Next row: K1, ssk, work to end of row. (31 sts)

Purl 1 row.

Rep last 2 rows until 21 sts remain, ending with a WS row.

Work even in St st for 40 more rows.

Place sts on holder.

Left Front

Work as for right front, reversing shaping.

Join fronts at back neck with Kitchener st.

Front Band

With RS facing, join yarn at lower marker on right front.

With smaller needle, pick up and k 110 sts to neck shaping marker, 124 sts around neck to neck shaping marker on left front, 109 sts to bottom marker. (343 sts)

Beg with a p row, work in St st for 5 rows.

Mark right front for 6 buttonholes, having first one ½ inch above lower edge and top one ½ inch below beg of neck shaping.

Buttonhole row (RS): [K to marker, bind off 2 sts] 6 times, k to end of row.

Next row: Purl, casting on 2 sts over each bound-off area.

Work in St st for 4 more rows.

Bind off.

Sew on buttons. ●

Firenze Necklace

Design by JoAnne Turcotte

You will want to make lots of these stylish necklaces for gifts, or to keep for yourself.

Skill Level

■□□□
BEGINNER

Size

One size fits most

Finished Measurement

Diameter: 7 inches

Materials

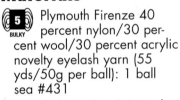 Plymouth Firenze 40 percent nylon/30 percent wool/30 percent acrylic novelty eyelash yarn (55 yds/50g per ball): 1 ball sea #431

- Size 10½ (6.5mm) 16-inch circular needles or size needed to obtain gauge

Gauge

14 sts = 4 inches/10cm in St st

To save time, take time to check gauge.

Necklace

Make 2

Cast on 60 sts very loosely. Join without twisting, pm between first and last st.

Work even in St st for 1½ inches.

Bind off loosely.

Finishing

With purl side facing outwards, sew cast-on sts to bound-off sts.

To wear, loop 1 necklace through another.

For alternate look, combine 2 necklaces of coordinating colors. ●

Garter Ridge Bag

Design by Lois S. Young

Here is a quick purse that will delight young and old alike. Make several to diversify your wardrobe.

Skill Level

BEGINNER

Finished Size

Approx 9 inches wide x 10 inches high

Materials

Plymouth Fantasy Naturale 100 percent mercerized cotton worsted weight yarn: (140 yds/100g per ball): 2 balls lime #5228 (A)

Plymouth Eros 100 percent nylon novelty eyelash yarn (165 yds/50g per ball): 2 balls green variegated #1924 (B)

- Size 9 (5.5mm) 16-inch circular needle or size needed to obtain gauge
- Stitch markers

Gauge

15 sts and 25 rnds = 4 inches/10cm in Garter Ridge pat

To save time, take time to check gauge.

Pattern Stitch

Garter Ridge

Rnd 1: K1, p35; rep from * around.

Rnds 2, 4, 8 and 10: P1, k35; rep from * around.

Rnds 3, 5, 7 and 9: Knit.

Rnd 6: Purl.

Rep Rnds 1–10 for pat.

Pattern Note

One strand of each yarn is held tog for entire purse.

Bag

Cast on 36 sts, pm, cast on 36 sts. (72 sts)

Join without twisting, pm between first and last st.

Work even in Garter Ridge pat for 50 rnds.

Rep Rnds 1 and 2, rep Rnd 1.

Eyelet rnd: *K2tog, yo; rep from * around.

[Work Rnds 1–2] 3 times.

Bind off purlwise.

Twisted Cord Ties
Make 2

Cut 2 4-yd strands each of A and B.

Loop yarn around a cup hook or doorknob, fold in half and hold all ends tog.

Holding yarn taut, twist until yarn begins to kink upon itself.

Grasp cut ends in one hand, hold middle of cord with other hand. Bring cut end to looped end.

Release middle, letting cord twist back on itself.

Remove loop from knob or hook, smooth any remaining kinks.

Knot each end loosely.

Finishing

Turn bag inside out and sew bottom tog, folding at garter st "seams."

Turn to right side.

Run 1 cord through each side of bag, leaving an end at each "seam."

Adjust cords evenly, and knot them together.

Trim ends. ●

Row 3: Sl 1, k to last st before gap, sl 1, k1, psso, k1, turn.

Row 4: Sl 1, k to last st before gap, p2tog, p 1, turn.

Rep Rows 3–4 until all heel flap sts have been worked.

Next row: Sl 1, k rem 11 (13, 15) sts of heel; with same needle, pick up and k

12 (14, 16) sts along edge of heel flap; with another needle, k sts of needle #2; with 3rd needle, pick up and k 12 (14, 16) sts along edge

of heel flap, then with same needle k 6 (7, 8) sts from first needle. Sts will be arranged as 18-20-18 (21-24-21, 24-32-24).

Knit 1 rnd.

Gussets

Rnd 1: Needle #1: K to last 3 sts, k2tog, k1.

Needle #2: Knit.

Needle #3: K1, sl 1, k1, psso, k to end of needle.

Rnd 2: Knit.

Rep Rnds 1–2 until there are 10 (12, 14) sts left on needles #1 and #3. Sts will be arranged as 10-20-10 (12-24-12, 14-32-14).

Large size only: Rearrange sts to 15-30-15 by slipping 1 st from each end of needle #2 to each of needles #1 and #3.

Foot

K every rnd until foot, when measured from back of heel, measures 2 (2¼, 2½) inches less than desired foot measurement.

Toe

With needle #3, k across sts of needle #1. Sts will be arranged on 2 needles as 20-20 (24-24, 30-30).

Rnd 1: [K1, sl 1, k1, psso, k to last 3 sts on needle, k2tog, k1] twice.

Rnd 2: Knit.

Rep Rnds 1–2 until there are 12 (12, 14) sts on each needle, ending with Rnd 1.

[Rep Rnd 1] 2 (2, 3) times more. (8 sts on each needle)

Weave toe sts tog, using Kitchener method.

Basic Cuff Variation (shown on man's sock)

Cast on 40 (48, 60) sts. Arrange sts on 3 dpn needles as follows: 10-20-10 (12-24-12, 14-32-14).

Work in k1, p1 ribbing until cuff measures 2½ inches.

Beg at ***, work as for mock cable sock. ●

Sweetheart Hat
Continued from page 138

Rnd 8: K1, p1 around.

Rnd 9: K2tog around. (10, 12 sts)

Cut yarn, leaving a 12-inch end. Draw end through rem sts twice.

Pull tightly and fasten on inside.

Tassel

Cut 3 strands of yarn, each 18 inches long.

Pull strands through top of hat and adjust evenly.

Using 2 strands for each group, braid strands for 6 inches.

Tie ends of braid into a knot.

Cut 11 strands of yarn, each 9

inches long. Set 1 strand aside.

Center 10 strands in rem yarn of braid. Tie braid ends around tassel strands.

Fold tassel strands in half and with rem strand of yarn, wrap strands tightly, ½ inch below fold.

Tie tightly, hiding all ends in tassel.

Trim tassel evenly. ●

Wraparound Purse Cover
Continued from page 142

If you bind off with k sts held tog, the p side will become the RS of the cover and you will have more eyelash showing. If you want less eyelash, bind off with the p sts held tog.

Join bottom of cover using 3-needle bind off.

Handles

With 2 strands of MC held tog, cast on 6 sts leaving a long end for later use in attaching handle.

Work in I-cord for desired length of handle.

Bind off.

Cut yarn, leaving a 12-inch length for attaching handle.

Finishing

Pull cover over purse.

With double strand of elastic thread, sew a row of running sts directly below MC band. Pull elastic tightly and fasten. MC band will curl naturally.

With first rnd of CC at top edge of purse, spread glue in a bead along top edge and secure cover firmly to purse.

Sew handles to cover at outer corners. Reinforce handles by sewing top edge of cover tog just inside join. ●

All Around the House

Using double-pointed and circular needles will help you create knitted projects to enhance every room of your home. Plymouth Yarn comes in so many different colors that you'll find it easy to match your decor.

Dazzling Prism Lace

Design by Bonnie Franz

This funky shade imitates the look of colorful beads on metal mesh.

Skill Level

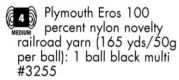
BEGINNER

Finished Size

Approx 6¼ inches high x 15 inches top circumference x 23 inches lower circumference

Materials

 Plymouth Eros 100 percent nylon novelty railroad yarn (165 yds/50g per ball): 1 ball black multi #3255

- Size 8 (5mm) 16-inch circular needle or size needed to obtain gauge
- Stitch marker

Gauge

14 sts and 24 rnds = 4 inches/10cm in Ridges pat

To save time, take time to check gauge.

Pattern Stitch

Ridges

Rnds 1–5: Knit.

Rnd 6: *Wrap yarn around needle twice, k next st; repeat from * around.

Rnd 7: Knit, dropping extra wraps.

Rep Rnds 1–7 for pat.

Note: *All rnds are worked on the WS.*

Lamp Shade Cover

Beg at top edge, cast on 53 sts. Join without twisting, pm between first and last st.

Knit 1 rnd, purl 1 rnd.

Work in Ridges pat for 28 rnds, inc 1 st before marker on every rnd. (81 sts)

Bind off knitwise.

Finishing

Turn cover inside out, this will be RS.

Cut 54 lengths of yarn, each 7 inches long.

Fold each strand in half an d attach to lower edge of shade, skipping every 3rd dropped st.

Trim fringe even. ●

Work even in garter st for 4 rnds.

Bind off.

Bolster

With CC, cast on 76 sts. Join without twisting, pm between first and last st.

Work in garter st for 4 rnds.

Change to MC and 3/1 Rib.

Work even until bolster measures 3 inches.

Eyelet rnd: K2tog, yo, k1, p1; rep from * around.

Work even until bolster measures 5½ inches.

Change to CC and work 4 rnds in garter st.

Change to MC and 3/1 Rib.

Work even in Rib pat until bolster measures 17 inches.

Change to CC and work 4 rnds in garter st.

Change to MC and 3/1 Rib.

Work even in Rib pat until bolster measures 20 inches.

Rep Eyelet rnd.

Work even in Rib pat until bolster measures 22½ inches.

Change to CC and work 4 rnds in garter st.

Bind off.

Finishing

Cut 4 strands of ribbon, each 24 inches long.

Thread 2 strands of ribbon through one Eyelet rnd.

Insert pillow form. Pull ribbon tightly and tie in bow.

Rep bow at opposite end. ●

Picket Fence Valance

Design by Liliane Dickinson

Flowers grow in front of a picket fence on a valance suitable for baby's room. For another look, use soft pastel colors for the floral embroidery.

Skill Level

INTERMEDIATE

Finished Size

Approx 15 x 36 inches

Materials

Plymouth Fantasy Naturale 100 percent cotton worsted weight yarn (140 yds/100g per skein): 4 skeins white #8001

- Size 8 (5mm) (2) 29-inch circular needles or size needed to obtain gauge
- Stitch markers
- Tapestry needle

Gauge

14 sts and 22 rows = 4 inches/10cm in St st

To save time, take time to check gauge.

Special Abbreviation

CDD (Centered Double Decrease): Sl 2 sts as if to k2tog, k1, pass 2 slipped sts over k st.

Pattern Stitches

A. Fence Lace (multiple of 13 + 7 sts)

Row 1 (RS): K3, *k7 [yo, k2tog] 3 times; rep from * to last 10 sts, k10.

Rows 2 and 4: K3, p7, *k6, p7; rep from * to last 3 sts, k3.

Row 3: K3, *k7 [k2tog, yo] 3 times; rep from * to last 10 sts, k10.

B. Tulip Lace (multiple of 8 + 7 sts)

Row 1 (RS): Knit.

Row 2 and all even-numbered rows: K3, p to last 3 sts, k3.

Row 3: K6, *yo, ssk, k6; rep from * to last 7 sts, yo, ssk, k5.

Row 5: K4, *k2tog, yo, k1, yo, ssk, k3; rep from * to last 9 sts, k2tog, yo, k1, yo, ssk, k4.

Row 7: Rep Row 3.

Row 9: Knit.

Row 11: K10, *yo, ssk, k6; rep from *, end last rep k3.

Row 13: K8, *k2tog, yo, k1, yo, ssk, k3; rep from * to last 5 sts, k5.

Row 15: Rep Row 11.

Row 16: Rep Row 2.

C. Checks

Row 1 (WS): K3, *k2, p2; rep from *, end last rep k5.

Row 2: Work all sts as they present themselves.

Row 3: K3, *p the knit stitches, k the purl stitches; rep from *, end last rep k3.

Row 4: Rep Row 2.

Rows 5 and 6: Rep Rows 1 and 2.

Valance

Cast on 130 sts.

Work in garter st for 6 rows.

Next row (WS): Work Row 2 of Fence Lace pat (if desired, pm at beg of each rep).

Work Rows 1–4 of Fence Lace pat; rep Rows 1 and 2.

Keeping first 3 sts and last 3 sts in garter st, work in St st for 6 rows.

Spiral Star Pillow

Design by Uyvonne Bigham

Make a pillow with a different pattern on each side, and you double your decorating options.

Skill Level

INTERMEDIATE

Finished Size

Approx 14 inches across

Materials

 Plymouth Galway 100 percent wool worsted weight yarn (210 yds/100g per skein): 1 skein soft white #01

- Size 8 (5mm) set of 5 double-pointed and 24-inch circular needles or size needed to obtain gauge
- Size H/8 (5mm) crochet hook
- Stitch markers
- 14-inch round purchased pillow form

Gauge

16 sts and 23 rnds = 4 inches/10cm in St st

To save time, take time to check gauge.

Pattern Notes

Change to longer needle when necessary.

Number in parentheses indicates st count for 1 section only.

Pillow

Side A (Large photo)

Make a sl knot, leaving a short tail. Hold knot with the LH and a needle in the RH. *Yo (1 stitch created), insert needle into lp of sl knot, wrap yarn around needle, and pull up a st (another st created). Rep from * until 16 sts have been cast on. After working a few rounds, pull on tail to tighten sl knot.

Divide sts evenly onto 4 dpn. Join without twisting, pm between first and last st.

Rnds 1–4: Knit.

Rnd 5: *Yo, k2, pm; rep from * around. (3 sts in each of 8 sections)

Rnd 6 and all even-numbered rnds: Knit.

Rnd 7: *Yo, k3; rep from * around. (4 sts)

Rnd 9: *Yo, k4; rep from * around. (5 sts)

Rnd 11: *Yo, k5; rep from * around. (6 sts)

Rnd 13: *Yo, k6; rep from * around. (7 sts)

Rnd 15: *Yo, k7; rep from * around. (8 sts)

Rnd 17: *Yo, k1, yo, k2tog, k5; rep from * around. (9 sts)

Rnd 19: *Yo, k1, [yo, k2tog] twice, k4; rep from * around. (10 sts)

Rnd 21: *Yo, k3, [yo, k2tog] twice, k3; rep from * around. (11 sts)

Rnd 23: *Yo, k5, [yo, k2tog] twice, k2; rep from * around. (12 sts)

Rnd 25: *Yo, k2, ssk, yo, k3, [yo, k2tog] twice, k1; rep from * around. (13 sts)

Rnd 27: *Yo, k2, [ssk, yo] twice, k3, [yo, k2tog] twice; rep from * around. (14 sts)

Rnd 29: *Yo, k2, [ssk, yo] 3 times, k3, yo, k2tog; rep from * around. (14 sts)

Rnd 31: *Yo, k2, [ssk, yo] 4 times, k3, yo, k2tog; rep from * around. (16 sts)

Rnd 33: *Yo, k2, [ssk, yo] 5 times, k4; rep from * around. (17 sts)

Rnd 35: *Yo, k2, [ssk, yo] 6

Continued on page 174

Cables Square & Round

Designs by Uyvonne Bigham

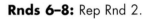

Matching pillows in different shapes will add a sophisticated touch to any room.

Skill Level

INTERMEDIATE

Finished Size

12 inches square or round

Materials

[4 MEDIUM] Plymouth Galway 100 percent wool worsted weight yarn (210 yds/100g per skein): 2 skeins light turquoise #111

- Size 8 (5mm) set of 5 double-pointed, 16- and 24-inch circular needles or size needed to obtain gauge
- Cable needle
- Stitch markers
- 12-inch square purchased pillow form
- 12-inch round purchased pillow form

Gauge

20 sts and 24 rnds = 4 inches/10cm in St st

To save time, take time to check gauge.

Special Abbreviation

C1F (Cable 1 Front): Sl next st to cn and hold in front, k2, k1 from cn.

C1B (Cable 1 Back): Sl next 2 sts to cn and hold in back, k1, k2 from cn.

C2F (Cable 2 Front): Sl next 2 sts to cn and hold in front, k2, k2 from cn.

C2B (Cable 2 Back): Sl next 2 sts to cn and hold in back, k2, k2 from cn.

Pattern Notes

For round pillow, change to larger needles when necessary.

Numbers in parentheses indicate st count for 1 section only.

Square Pillow

With crochet hook, ch 55.

With shorter circular needle, pick up and k 54 sts from top lp of ch, turn work and pick up 54 sts from bottom lp of ch. This will form the closed bottom of pillow. Pm between first and last st. (108 sts)

Rnd 1: Knit.

Rnd 2–4: *K7, [p1, k4] twice, p1, k3, p2, k8, p2, k3, p1, [k4, p1] twice, k7; rep from * once.

Rnd 5: *K7, p1, C2B, p6, C1B, p2, C2B, C2F, p2, C1F, p6, C2F, p1, k7; rep from * once.

Rnds 6–8: Rep Rnd 2.

Rnd 9: *K7, p1, C2B, p1, k4, p1, C1B, p2, k8, p2, C1F, p1, k4, p1, C2F, p1, k7; rep from * once.

[Rep Rnds 2–9] 8 times more.

Bind off in pat.

Finishing

Insert pillow form, sew top opening.

Round Pillow

Make 2 halves alike

Make a sl knot, leaving a short tail. Hold knot with the LHand a needle in the RH. *Yo (1 st created), insert needle into lp of slip knot, wrap yarn around needle, and pull up a st (another st created). Rep from * until 16 sts have been cast on. After working a few rounds, pull on tail to tighten sl knot. Divide sts evenly onto 4 dpn.

Rnds 1 and 2: Knit.

Rnd 3: *[K1, yo] twice, pm; rep from * around. (4 sts)

Rnd 4: *K4, yo; rep from * around. (5 sts)

Rnd 5: *K4, p1; rep from * around.

Rnd 6: *K4, yo, p1; rep from * around. (6 sts)

Rnd 7: *C2B, p2; rep from * around.

Rnd 8: *K4, yo, p2; rep from * around. (7 sts)

Rnd 9: *K4, p3; rep from * around.

Rnd 10: *K4, yo, p3; rep from * around. (8 sts)

Rnd 11: *C2B, p4; rep from * around.

Rnd 12: *K4, p1, yo, p3; rep from * around. (9 sts)

Rnd 13: *K4, p5; rep from * around.

Rnd 14: *K4, p2, yo, p3; rep from * around. (10 sts)

Rnd 15: *C2B, p6; rep from * around.

Rnd 16: *K4, p6; rep from * around.

Rnd 17: *K4, p3, yo, p3; rep from * around. (11 sts)

Rnd 18: *K4, p3, k1, p3; rep from * around.

Rnd 19: *C2B, p3, yo, k1, yo, p3; rep from * around. (13 sts)

Rnds 20–22: *K4, p3, k3, p3; rep from * around.

Rnd 23: *C2B, p3, yo, k3, yo, p3; rep from * around. (15 sts)

Rnds 24–26: *K4, p3, k5, p3; rep from * around.

Rnd 27: *C2B, p3, yo, k5, yo, p3; rep from * around. (17 sts)

Rnds 28–30: *K4, p3, k7, p3; rep from * around.

Rnd 31: *C4B, p3, yo, k7, yo, k3; rep from * around. (19 sts)

Rnd 32: *K4, p3, k9, p3; rep from * around. (152 sts total)

Place sts on spare circular needle or holder.

Finishing

Pull sl knot at cast-on edge tightly to close center opening on each piece.

With WS tog, join both halves using 3-needle bind-off, inserting pillow form when approx 6 sections have been joined. Complete bind off. ●

Outback Rug

Design by Joanne Turcotte

Step onto this soft wool rug and your feet will say, "Thank you."

Skill Level

EASY

Finished Size

Approx 36 inches in diameter

Materials

[4] MEDIUM Plymouth Outback Wool 100 percent virgin wool worsted weight yarn (370 yds/200g per hank): 4 hanks grape #959

- Size 10 (6mm) double-pointed, 16-, 24- and 32-inch circular needles or size needed to obtain gauge
- Size G/6 (4mm) crochet hook

Gauge

16 sts and 32 rnds = 4 inches/10cm in garter st

To save time, take time to check gauge.

Rug

With dpn, cast on 6 sts. Divide evenly onto 3 needles. Join without twisting, pm between first and last st.

Rnd 1: K into front and back of each st. (12 sts)

Rnd 2 and all even-numbered rounds: Purl.

Rnd 3: *K1, k into front and back of next st, pm; rep from * around. (18 sts)

Rnd 5: *K2, k into front and back of next st; rep from * around. (24 sts).

Rnd 7: *K3, k into front and back of next st; rep from * around. (30 sts).

Continue to inc every other rnd as established until there are 60 sts between markers, changing to longer needles as necessary and ending with Rnd 2.

Edging

With crochet hook, *ch 6, insert hook into next 3 sts on LH needle and sc them tog; rep from * around. Join with sl st.

Block to soft hexagon shape, flattening edging slightly. ●

Ruffled Candle Mats

Designs by Lynda K. Roper

Take your pick of two sizes and weights for these candle accessories.

Skill Level

EASY

Finished Size

6 (8) inches diameter

Materials

4 MEDIUM Plymouth Wildflower D.K. 51 percent cotton/49 percent acrylic DK weight yarn (136 yds/ 50g per ball): 1 ball light teal #15 (A)

3 LIGHT Plymouth Fantasy Naturale 100 percent mercerized cotton worsted weight yarn (140 yds/ 100g per skein): 1 ball teal #8021 (B)

- Size 5 (3.75mm) double-pointed, 16- and 24-inch circular needles or size needed to obtain gauge for smaller candle mat

- Size 8 (5mm) double-pointed, 16- and 24-inch circular needles or size needed to obtain gauge for larger candle mat

- Stitch marker

Gauge

For smaller candle mat:
5 sts and 7 rnds = 1 inch/ 2.5cm in St st with smaller needles

For larger candle mat:
4 sts and 5 rnds = 1 inch/ 2.5cm in St st with larger needles

To save time, take time to check gauge.

Pattern Notes

Directions are the same for both sizes. Needles determine finished size of candle mat.

Change to shorter needles when necessary.

Candle Mat

Beg at outer edge with A (B) and smaller (larger) circular needle, cast on 200 sts. Join without twisting, pm between first and last st.

Rnds 1–4: Knit.

Rnd 5: *K1, drop next st off needle; rep from * around. (100 sts)

Rnd 6: Ssk around. (50 sts)

Rnd 7: Knit.

Rnd 8: *K3, ssk; rep from * around. (40 sts)

Rnd 9: Knit.

Rnd 10: *K2, ssk; rep from * around. (30 sts)

Rnd 11: Knit.

Rnd 12: *K1, ssk; rep from * around. (20 sts)

Rnd 13: Knit.

Rnd 14: Ssk around. (10 sts)

Cut yarn, leaving a 12-inch end.

Draw through rem sts twice, secure on WS.

Totally unravel all dropped sts for ruffled edge. ●

Starburst Table Mat

Design by Sue Childress

Add sparkle to your table with this out-of-the-ordinary shaped mat.

Skill Level

EASY

Finished Size

Approx 16 inches diameter

Materials

- Plymouth Fantasy Naturale 100 percent mercerized cotton worsted weight yarn (140 yds/100g per skein): 1 skein blue/green #9936
- Size 7 (4.5mm) double-pointed, 16- and 24-inch circular needles or size needed to obtain gauge
- Stitch marker

Gauge

12 sts and 22 rnds = 4 inches/10cm in St st after blocking

To save time, take time to check gauge.

Pattern Note

Change to longer needles when necessary.

Table Mat

With dpn, cast on 8 sts. Divide evenly onto 4 needles. Join without twisting, pm between first and last st.

Rnds 1, 3, 5 and 7: *Yo, k1; rep from * around.

Rnds 2, 4, 6, 8, 10 and 12: Knit.

Rnd 9: *K2, yo; rep from * around. (192 sts)

Rnd 11: *K4, yo; rep from * around. (240 sts)

Rnd 13: *K2tog, k1; rep from * around. (160 sts)

Rnd 14: Purl.

Rnd 15: *P2tog, p3; rep from * around. (128 sts)

Rnd 16: Purl.

Rnd 17: *P2tog, p2; rep from * around. (96 sts)

Rnds 18–21: Knit

Rnd 22: *K6, yo; rep from * around. (112 sts)

Rnds 23, 25, 27 and 29: Knit.

Rnd 24: *K7, yo; rep from * around. (128 sts)

Rnd 26: *K8, yo; rep from * around. (144 sts)

Rnd 28: *K4, yo, k5, yo; rep from * around. (176 sts)

Rnd 30: *K5, yo, k6, yo; rep from * around. (208 sts)

Rnds 31–32: Knit.

Bind off purlwise.

Wet-block, pulling points into place. ●

Geometric Zigzags

Designs by JC Briar

Zigzags and flags give this place mat a Southwestern feel.

Skill Level

EASY

Finished Sizes

Place Mat: Approx 17 x 11 inches

Coaster: Approx 4 inches square

Materials

Plymouth Wildflower D.K. 51 percent cotton/ 49 percent acrylic DK weight yarn (136 yds/50g per ball): 2 balls gold #78

- Size 5 (3.75mm) set of 5 double-pointed, 16- and 24-inch circular needles or size needed to obtain gauge
- Stitch markers
- Tapestry needle

Gauge

22 sts and 36 rnds = 4 inches/10cm in St st

To save time, take time to check gauge.

Pattern Notes

Pinhole Cast-On: Make a sl knot, leaving a short tail. Hold knot in LH and needle in RH. *Yo (1 st created), insert needle into lp of sl knot, wrap yarn around needle, and pull up a st (another st created). Rep from * until required amount of sts have been cast on. After working a few rounds, pull on tail to tighten sl knot.

Change to longer needles when necessary for place mat.

Place Mat

With shorter circular needle, cast on 60 sts, leaving an 18-inch end for later use in sewing center tog. Join without twisting.

Rnd 1: [Pm, k3, pm, k27] twice.

Rnd 2: [K1, yo, k to 1 st before marker, yo, k1] 4 times. (68 sts)

Rnd 3: Purl.

Rnd 4: [K1, yo, k1, (yo, k2tog) to 1 st before marker, yo, k1] 4 times. (76 sts)

Rnd 5: Knit.

Rnds 6–9: Rep Rnds 2–5. (92 sts)

Rnd 10: Rep Rnd 2. (100 sts)

Rnd 11: Purl.

Rnd 12: Rep Rnd 2. (108 sts)

Rnd 13 and all odd-numbered rnds through Rnd 49: Knit.

Rnd 14: [K1, yo, k1, (k2, p4, k2tog, yo, k4) to 1 st before marker, yo, k1] 4 times. (116 sts)

Rnd 16: [K1, yo, k3, (p4, k2tog, yo, k6) to 1 st before marker, yo, k1] 4 times. (124 sts)

Rnd 18: [K1, yo, k3, (p4, k2tog, yo, k6) to 3 sts before marker, k2, yo, k1] 4 times. (132 sts)

Rnd 20: [K1, yo, k2, (k6, yo, ssk, p4) to 6 sts before marker, k5, yo, k1] 4 times. (140 sts)

Rnd 22: [K1, yo, k4, (k6, yo, ssk, p4) to 6 sts before marker, k5, yo, k1] 4 times. (148 sts)

Rnd 24: [K1, yo, k6, (k6, yo, ssk, p4) to 6 sts before marker, k5, yo, k1] 4 times. (156 sts)

Rnd 26: K1, yo, k9, (p4, k2tog, yo, k6) to 5 sts before marker, k4, yo, k1] 4 times. (164 sts)

Rnd 28: [K1, yo, k9, (p4, k2tog, yo, k6) to 7 sts before marker, k6, yo, k1] 4 times. (172 sts)

Rnd 30: [K1, yo, k9, (p4, k2tog, yo, k6) to 9 sts before marker, k8, yo, k1] 4 times. (180 sts)

Rnd 32: [K1, yo, k2, (yo, ssk, p4, k6) to 6 sts before marker, k5, yo, k1] 4 times. (188 sts)

Rnd 34: [K1, yo, k4, (yo, ssk, p4, k6) to 6 sts before marker, k5, yo, k1] 4 times. (196 sts)

Rnd 36: [K1, yo, k6, (yo, ssk, p4, k6) to 6 sts before marker, k5, yo, k1] 4 times. (204 sts)

Rnds 38–49: Rep Rnds 14–25. (252 sts)

Rnd 50: [K1, yo, k to 1 st before marker, yo, k1] 4 times. (260 sts)

Rnd 51: Purl.

Rnd 52: [K1, yo, k1, (yo, k2tog) to 1 st before marker, yo, k1] 4 times. (268 sts)

Rnd 53: Knit.

Rnd 54: Rep Rnd 50. (276 sts)

Rnd 55: Purl.

Bind off loosely.

Fold cast-on edge in half and sew tog.

Coaster

Cast on 8 sts using pinhole method. Divide evenly onto 4 needles. Join without twisting,

pm between first and last st.

Rnd 1: *K1, yo, k1; rep from * around. (12 sts)

Rnd 2: Knit.

Rnd 3: *K1, yo, k1, yo, k1; rep from * around. (20 sts)

Rnd 4: Purl.

Rnd 5: *K1, yo, k1, [yo, k2tog] to last st on needle, yo, k1; rep from * around. (28 sts)

Rnd 6: Knit.

Rnd 7: *K1, yo, k to last st on needle, yo, k1; rep from * around. (36 sts)

Rnd 8: Purl.

Rnds 9–20: [Rep Rnds 5–8] 3 times. (84 sts)

Bind off loosely. ●

Spiral Star Pillow

Continued from page 162

times, k4; rep from * around. (19 sts)

Rnd 37: *Yo, k2, [ssk, yo] 7 times, k2; rep from * around. (19 sts)

Rnd 39: *Yo, k2, [ssk, yo] 8 times, k1; rep from * around. (20 sts)

Rnd 40 Knit.

Work in garter st for 4 rnds.

Bind off knitwise.

Side B (Small photo)

Make a sl knot, leaving a short tail. Work 16 sts into knot as for Side A. Divide evenly onto 4 dpn. Join without twisting, pm between first and last st.

Rnds 1–4: Knit.

Rnd 5: *Yo, k2, pm; rep from * around. (3 sts)

Rnd 6 and all even-numbered rnds: Knit.

Rnd 7: *Yo, k3; rep from * around. (4 sts)

Rnd 9: *Yo, k4; rep from * around. (5 sts)

Continue to work in this man-

ner, knitting all even-numbered rnds and having 1 more st in each section on odd-numbered rnds until there are 20 sts between markers. (160 sts total)

Work in garter st for 4 rnds.

Bind off knitwise.

Finishing

Pull sl knot at cast-on edge tightly to close center opening on each piece.

Sew both pieces tog, leaving an opening for inserting form.

Insert pillow form and sew rem of opening. ●

Standard Abbreviations

[ ] ....work instructions within brackets as many times as directed

( ) ....work instructions within parentheses in the place directed

** ....repeat instructions following the asterisks as directed

* ....repeat instructions following the single asterisk as directed

" ....inch(es)

approx ....approximately

beg ....begin/beginning

CC...........contrasting color

ch ....chain stitch

cm ....centimeter(s)

cn ....cable needle

dec ....decrease/decreases/decreasing

dpn ....double pointed needle(s)

g.............gram

inc ....increase/increases/increasing

k.............knit

k2tog ......knit 2 stitches together

LH ....left hand

lp(s).........loop(s)

m ....meter(s)

M1..........make one stitch

MC ....main color

mm..........millimeter(s)

oz ....ounce(s)

p.............purl

pat(s).......pattern(s)

pm ....place marker

p2tog ......purl 2 stitches together

psso ....pass slipped stitch over

rem ....remain/remaining

rep..........repeat(s)

rev St st ...reverse stockinette stitch

RH ....right hand

rnd(s).......rounds

RS...........right side

skp..........slip, knit, pass stitch over—one stitch decreased

sk2p........slip 1, knit 2 together, pass slip stitch over the knit 2 together; 2 stitches have been decreased

sl ....slip

sl1k.........slip 1 knitwise

sl1p.........slip 1 purlwise

sl st ....slip stitch(es)

ssk ....slip, slip, knit these 2 stitches together—a decrease

st(s) ....stitch(es)

St st.........stockinette stitch/stocking stitch

tbl ....through back loop

tog ....together

WS ....wrong side

wyib........with yarn in back

wyif.........with yarn in front

yd(s) ....yard(s)

yfwd........yarn forward

yo ....yarn over

Special Thanks

We would like to thank Plymouth Yarn Co. for providing all the yarn used in this book. We really appreciate the help provided by Uyvonne Bigham and the Plymouth staff throughout the publishing process. It's been great working with them. We also thank the talented knitting designers whose work is featured in this collection.